GOTTLIEB

The gay tapes

DATE DUE			
NOV			
12-5-2005			

The
Gay
Tapes

The Gay Tapes

A CANDID DISCUSSION ABOUT MALE HOMOSEXUALITY

David I. Gottlieb, M.D.

𝔰𝔇

STEIN AND DAY/*Publishers*/New York

First published in 1977
Copyright © 1977 by David I. Gottlieb, M.D.
All rights reserved
Printed in the United States of America
Stein and Day/*Publishers*/Scarborough House,
Briarcliff Manor, N.Y. 10510

Library of Congress Cataloging in Publication Data

Gottlieb, David, 1929-
The gay tapes.

1. Homosexuality, Male. I. Title.
RC558.G68   616.8'5834'09   76-57987
ISBN 0-8128-2262-5

To my wife, Donna,
and my daughters,
Marci and Juli

Preface

Written and spoken opinions are not absolute. People are ambivalent and inconsistent. They are contradictory and emotional. They rationalize and intellectualize. If we are not patient we sometimes jump to ugly, simplistic, self-serving conclusions. Keep this in mind as you read this book.

I am greatly indebted to my wife Donna for her assistance in writing and to my daughters for their forbearance and trustworthiness during the preparation of the work. Without my collaborators, real but anonymous, the book could not have been written in this candid way.

Los Angeles, California
March, 1977

Contents

Contents

The
Gay
Tapes

Introduction

I am a psychiatrist and psychoanalyst with a practice that has ranged from treating children to treating the elderly. As a psychoanalyst I have dealt in the most intensive way possible with the deepest elements of the unconscious. I have also treated people very supportively and superficially with or without medication, and for fifteen years have taught adult and child psychiatry to psychiatrists in training.

This volume emerged from my treatment of several male homosexual patients. I find that there is no body of knowledge to help the male gay adapt successfully to society. He is subject to immense amounts of misinformation from fellow gays and the general community, and, because he is gay, the information is rife with sensationalism and prejudice. Not only is the homosexual affected by this ignorance, but also doctors and psychiatrists, sociologists and teachers, and last but not least, parents have no idea of what goes on in the lives and minds of roughly 3-to-5 percent of our population—the gays.

The need is here, and I want to fill it in a useful way. Surveys and statistics have little meaning to the individual. I decided to work with few people, in depth, rather than superficially with a large number, stressing therefore, qualitative, not quantitative information.

To initiate this work, I contacted Andy Andrews, whom I have known for thirty-five years. In 1964 I was surprised by an urgent call from him. He blurted out that he was gay, uncomfortably admitting something that he thought I knew all along. Actually, the thought had never entered my mind. I gave him a psychiatric referral, thinking perhaps his difficulties would be resolved if he could be "altered" to be like me. Suffice it to say that the alteration didn't happen, and we saw very little of each other until Andy's parents died and I called him to express my sympathy.

I told him that I wanted to write a book about homosexual adjustment and needed his help. I know that a psychiatrist has no license to delve into the lives and thoughts of people who are not his patients, particularly if they are friends. However, Andy's attitude was one of delight, relief, and even excitement.

As the work proceeded I contacted two other gay men, Jim Price and Bill Weber, whose ideas and feelings I compare and contrast with Andrews' throughout. All three are men who have been concerned with their appearance and have actively worked at building and maintaining their physiques. None of them is obviously gay either in speech, gesture, gait, or dress. Our taped discussions provide the matrix of the book. My wife added another dimension by

Introduction

suggesting questions only a woman would have. In addition to the dialogue, each chapter contains my introductory comments, interpretations, and conclusions.

Homosexuality is no longer considered a disease by the American Psychiatric Association. However, there is still controversy among professionals regarding the causes of homosexuality. This book does not deal with causality. The causality controversy, although interesting and, one hopes, productive, doesn't help the gay unless he *wants* to change. It is saying, "Unless you want to be straight I can't help you with your problems."

If a man presents himself at my office and announces that he is gay and does not want to be straight, I feel obligated to treat him for whatever is bothering him. I will not superimpose my sexual preferences on him overtly or covertly. I tried it many years ago and it didn't work. My gay patients were rightfully unhappy with me. Psychiatry is the only specialty in medicine where the patient must dictate the limits and direction of his own treatment. In other words, *he* is the most active participant in treatment.

Three-fourths of the way through the discussions Andrews and I became depressed and couldn't complete the night's work. When I saw him the next day, we greeted each other with the same statement, "Did I have a nightmare last night!"

I dreamed that I had the leading role in a major play and was totally unprepared. The play started and I heard the actors on stage. My anxiety grew to panic, and I awoke, depressed and frightened.

Andy dreamed that he was in a terrifying maze of train tracks. Without warning, other trains appeared and collided. He became two people in one: an engineer of one of

15

the colliding trains and a detached newscaster describing the event. He was responsible for the accident and at the same time detached from it so that he was immobilized. He awoke in a cold sweat.

Dreams may have many interpretations but ours, at this time, had particular significance.

I symbolically chose to perform in an area where I am inexperienced—acting. I actually prefer having a low profile. Maybe I should stay with treating my psychiatric patients and not risk criticism by doing research and writing.

Andy, on the other hand, does not feel competent to speak for all gays and finds himself literally split between being a participant and an observer.

Any of the conclusions and suggestions made here are open to your criticism, disagreement, and rejection. I kept absolutes to a minimum. Maybe some of the answers will be the reader's. Maybe some questions will be his. This is a scientific inquiry, and the first step in any science is to ask questions.

1

Early Sex Information and Experiences

Sexuality emerges laboriously through infancy and childhood to finally express itself in the adult. Understanding it baffles most people. We repress our early childhood experiences as well as the sexual information we were given, and because we see our childhood through adult eyes, looking back can be troublesome and emotionally embarrassing. My focus here is adult, gay adaptation to life, sexually and socially. In this section I am emphasizing childhood and adolescent sexual exposure and its effect on the adult gay. I repeat, I am *not* discussing the *causes* of homosexuality.

Gays and straights are subject to similar misconceptions and misadventures. My own early sexual education can be summarized in one word: none. Worse, it was an education in fear. At age fifteen I waited in line in Minnesota's sub-zero weather to see a 1940s version of an X-rated movie consisting of scenes of a bloody childbirth. There was a nurse on duty in case someone got sick. If you didn't get sick from the childbirth scenes, your fantasies were stimulated by movies of syphilitic cripples. For a month afterward I felt uneasy around girls. I was afraid that if I exercised my sexual feelings toward them they would go through a bloody childbirth and die. Or maybe I would get syphilis and suffer a painful, humiliating death. Sex was presented as a sin that had to be punished. The "sin" of sex was always heterosexual. Homosexuality was too unthinkable to be considered.

Early in life boys are forbidden to fool around with girls. They are told that it isn't nice to play "doctor" and investigate each other's bodies. Between nine and fourteen boys tell dirty jokes to each other, compare genital sizes and erections, and engage in body-contact play. This is the age when boys pin up pictures of male movie stars and athletes. Their whole orientation is directed toward the male ideal and everyone expects them to behave this way. Then they have to switch their interests to the opposite sex. If they continue to have homosexual interests they're considered peculiar.

Bill Weber is charismatic. He appears to have everything under control. He is lithe and powerfully built, with immense shoulders and hands that remind me of Michelangelo's *David*. He has a craggy, asymetrical, masculine face. His voice weakens at times of stress, which gave me the first indication that he is not made of granite. He is also indecisive, melancholic, and impulsive. He speaks of conscience with tears in his eyes and yet this most masculine man has glaring defects in his emotional ethics and morality.

Early Sex Information and Experiences

Bill would like to be a three-dimensional man with a past, present, and future, but he is a man of the moment. The immediate situation determines his reactions and interactions with people. He is entertaining, verbal, and humorous, but there is a jaded, almost dissipated quality about him. He comes on strong, with direct, overwhelming opinions but these opinions wither under fire and he runs away. He is fascinating when caught because not only does he talk, he acts. He's colorful, but he expends tremendous effort running from the threat of his own warmth and kindness.

Bill describes his childhood sexual conflicts with disarming sensitivity.

GOTTLIEB: The point I want to make is that the homosexual experience is frowned upon in mid and late adolescence, while in childhood and early adolescence homosexuality is okay. There's no guilt associated with playing with boys, but there is guilt in playing around with girls.

WEBER: I guess this is what really happened to me. I was so scared. You're around this homosexuality, but all of a sudden you're expected to switch. So fast.

GOTTLIEB: That's right.

WEBER: I didn't prefer to switch. There was this aura, this thing on the street. It was even stronger then. All of a sudden I couldn't say I'd rather go out with my friend Johnny. No, no no. I shouldn't go out with him. I should go out with a girl.

GOTTLIEB: Yes.

WEBER: Before it was that they'd beat the hell out of you for touching a little girl, but now all of a sudden . . .

GOTTLIEB: Now all of a sudden you're supposed to be interested in girls' bodies.

WEBER: Yes. I lived in the country and we used to sleep over at one another's house. All of a sudden my buddy and I weren't allowed to sleep next to each other. My mother said to me when I was an adolescent, "No, son, you can't do that. You're too old for that."

GOTTLIEB: Yes.

WEBER: She all of a sudden transferred over. I was confused. I didn't know why. I didn't understand why this quick change. I really never thought about that.

It is stressful enough to have to make the switch, but it must be terribly painful to pretend to do so when your heart is not in it. What conflict must exist in the mind of a young man who cannot. He is different. Where does he go?

I asked Andrews about his experiences in coming out.

ANDREWS: Sex education ignored the homosexual. It made me feel guilty about what I didn't know I was. I didn't come out. I stumbled out.

My children think Andy is cute. He is very neat and has an expressive, malleable face. His humor is salty and sometimes biting. He calls my children "adult molesters." Andy is also too compassionate and seems to pick up others' problems and make them his own. He is not totally unselfish, however, since he will unload difficulties on others with great articulate skill and a certain demanding quality.

He is a nag, but he is so funny that one excuses him for it.

He can be tough in business when people are at a distance, but very soft in close contact. He is a collector and putterer and an excellent cook. All in all he seems to muddle through life with amazing productivity and inventiveness.

I asked Bill Weber about the sexual instructions he had received. Weber appeared so adequate and ruggedly masculine that I had a difficult time perceiving him as a child curious about sexuality.

WEBER: You can guess it wasn't too good. I don't think I had any sex education at all. We had an old, funny book from about 1918 with very frightening advice and I used to sneak out and read that. I don't think I got any kind of sexual arousal out of it, yet at the same time I was very sexually active in early childhood. I was constantly being caught with little girls and punished, but no explanation was given for why I shouldn't be doing this or that. Spying on me and making me apprehensive was my mother's main job. When I came out, I was extremely naive. I knew nothing about homosexuality.

Jim Price is a magnificently handsome man whom people turn to look at. He is naive and quite absentminded. For a man so good looking he is extremely warm. He is intelligent and thoughtful, but for some reason was usually nervous with me. He speaks little, listens well. He is not a comedian like Andrews, but does have a sense of humor. He is scholarly and well read, and although disorganized, he is a superb professional. He is not charismatic in the flashy way that Weber is.

Jim also had very little in the way of sexual information as a youth, and what little there was, was negative.

GOTTLIEB: What about sexual information as a kid?

PRICE: Nothing. Not even mentioned, except in the worst sense. I remember asking my dad something when I was in the eighth grade. I still think the world of him, but he was very restrictive. I think he really was very frightened of sexuality himself. My mother gave me some religious instructions which made me very uncomfortable. I do remember something now about sexual activity. My father caught me masturbating and said, "Next time I see you doing that, I'm going to take you down to the doctor and get it all straightened out." There's something about that one experience that made me forever repress any feeling of wanting to discuss anything personal with him.

Each of these situations is obvious. There is limited instruction for the young person. There are no guidelines. When the gay discovers himself, it is logical that he is frightened by his own impulses.

How good are instructions anyway? It seems that even now sexual instructions are usually given in the negative: Don't get pregnant, don't get VD; and don't embarrass anyone. As a partial result of this many people separate sex from love and do not understand the fusion of the two.

Without any frame of reference, first experiences can be confusing. In his particularly expressive way, Andrews described furtively playing around with a good friend of his, a straight. Both of them felt the sexual pressures, but Andrews had a secret, mixed bag of fantasies in addition.

ANDREWS: I think a lot of guys have homosexual moments but the straights drop them when they start making out with girls. So straights can get away with a little homosexuality early in life and forget it later.

GOTTLIEB: How did you feel about that early sex with straights?

ANDREWS: I felt great and none of us talked much about it later. Any repeated contacts were just to relieve pressures and weren't discussed.

GOTTLIEB: Did you feel you were gay then?

ANDREWS: I felt different but just as masculine.

Andrews lost his usual articulate way of communicating when he tried to describe his early experiences. They were clouded with confusion about do's and don't's and all subjected to heterosexual society's pressure on the teenager to engage in no sex at all. For straights, homosexual experiences were not official sex and did not count, but for Andy they were beginning to count and he was chalking up numbers.

Weber was more specific about himself, maintaining that he had no homosexual experiences prior to college.

WEBER: The first time I had contact with another guy I was a senior in college. It was a disaster. I was scared and frightened. I didn't know what it meant. I didn't know where to turn. I went to the library and took out books on homosexuality. Later, after looking at all those books, I learned nothing and I was doubly confused.

Price indicated that he was not really concerned about teenage homosexual activities because he'd had very few.

Where a person grows up may have a great deal to do with how he expresses himself heterosexually and homosexually. A small community may be more repressive than a larger one. Weber was brought up in a small town and felt very strongly about early homosexual experiences.

WEBER: Being the only homosexual in a small town is a curse. The pressure is terrible. In a big city you can get lost. You can find a group of homosexuals and find some companionship. In a small town everyone notices everything and they focus on you.

Of course, this is why gay people can't wait to leave their hometowns and come to places like Los Angeles and New York.

GOTTLIEB: Your first sexual experiences were homosexual?

WEBER: No. They were hetrosexual. There was no outlet when I was young for homosexual experiences—or even thoughts.

In a long discussion with Andrews I pointed out that there is a predictable period of homosexuality in childhood and early adolescence. It includes sports—individual and body-contact—boys' clubs, and fraternities. Paralleling these activities is a secret fascination for one another's physical attributes. This may spill over into some overt homosexual activity. Many straight adults are terrified by memories of their mixed sexual impulses—expressed and unexpressed—from this period. During adolescence an affectionate, loving, and sexual relationship with a member of the same sex does not make one a homosexual, yet many heterosexuals fear they are really homosexual just because of it. Andrews responded rather impishly to this point by saying, "One swallow does not a cocksucker make."

Bridging the gap between child and adult sexuality is an experience that is extremely difficult for everyone. Many homosexuals had repressed, nonsexual, furtive childhoods. Perhaps they were very good boys who had unspeakable fantasies and thoughts that sooner or later burst into instinctual feeling, rebellion, and sexual preoccupation. They were ready to be brought out, to be seduced by a gay for the first time.

Andrews was skeptical about a common misconception that gays are *brought* out by other gays.

ANDREWS: Nobody brings you out. You bring yourself out. You alone are responsible for coming out.

GOTTLIEB: It's necessary for some gays to believe they've been brought out in order to diminish their guilt. It's like saying, "The devil made me do it," or, "I was drunk."

ANDREWS: That's a cop-out.

I then asked Andy if as a child he saw himself as a real boy or a sissy.

Andrews answered that he never liked to participate in contact sports or even to watch them. His father was profoundly disappointed by this and repeatedly urged him to change. "Dad wanted me to be a jock, but the only sport that interested me was a noncontact sport like body building—which of course led to another kind of contact sport."

As I pursued the question even further, Andrews lost his sense of humor and felt pressured. He avoided my questions by pointing out that many professional athletes are gay. I did not accept that. I was not interested in justifying homosexuality or heterosexuality. I wanted to know how the gay perceives himself even in retrospect. Andrews, usually the controlled intellectual, became somewhat angry.

ANDREWS: Don't generalize about gays. Each evolves uniquely. Some guys are active. Look, I know this very big, well-built stud, a high school and college football hero—built like a brick shithouse. But he's passive! He thinks he's macho but he's only fooling himself. He's gay—more gay than me. Does that answer your question?

Under considerable pressure from my questioning, Andrews stated that he went through adolescent dating with great difficulty and was very concerned about getting laid and making out with girls.

This discussion underlines a common clinical experience I have had. Most people start out to approximate what appears to them to be the norm. They feel they should go out with the gang and be part of the group. Even in a city you are always within a small group of peers, and peer pressure is the strongest force in the development of the adolescent. Peer pressure equals conformity. This is the origin of the put-down "queer" instead of "gay" to describe homosexuals. If you do not do what the group does, you are queer, odd, an outsider.

There is a facet of this attitude that I share with Andrews. We were both jealous of the good-looking guy who made out a lot.

ANDREWS: I really envied that guy. I hated him and I loved him because he was successfully straight. There could be nothing gay about him. If I could have him sexually, my own maleness seemed to be increased.

I wanted his beautiful girl friend. Andrews did too, but he also wanted the guy.

It is not a matter of recruiting a person into gay life. It is a matter of vicariously enjoying the heterosexual experience. It's all very mixed up, to seek maleness—and ironically, heterosexuality—through homosexuality.

The question then becomes, how does the homosexual bridge the gap? How does he feel about being involved with a man rather than a woman in a sexual embrace?

Labeling myself a bona fide heterosexual, this is one area that is most difficult for me to comprehend. I can understand the mechanical sexual activities, the reaching of an orgasm through various homosexual acts, but it is the affectionate, warm interchange that seems to be very difficult. What do gay people do?

In my own psychoanalysis I remember once being very

uncomfortable in discussing this concept. My analyst pointed out, "But, Dr. Gottlieb, you've had experience with this kind of thing." I turned to him from the couch and said, "I don't understand." He said, "Didn't you kiss your father?" I was shocked by the vivid impact of that remark. Of course I had a very strong, affectionate relationship with my father. I looked forward to embracing him and kissing him even when I returned home from medical school. Yet I had not equated this with the affectionate interaction between homosexuals.

Here Weber sadly recited his experience with his father.

WEBER: All through life I never touched my father. I was never allowed to even shake hands with him. Everything was at a distance. Everything was very formal. I found myself wishing to be close to him. Now he is a very sick man and there is a closer relationship. There is warmth. He does want some contact.

For Andrews, expressing physical affection was very difficult.

ANDREWS: I think I've already told you how hard it was for me to kiss a man for the first time—to express affection, even symbolically. That was a mind blower.

GOTTLIEB: I have to agree with you that to me the concept of kissing a male is very difficult.

ANDREWS: That was the worst part. I could see all the sexual activity without the expression of interest or affection, without the buildup of tenderness that kissing means. It seemed feminine. Two men embracing. Take an extreme concept: two men, two businessmen—two square people—

simply holding hands and showing affection. I couldn't take it.

GOTTLIEB: Did your father ever allow kissing?

ANDREWS: To a point, but there came a certain time in childhood when I couldn't kiss Dad. I did a purposeful embrace and buss on the cheek for a time into adulthood, but I dropped it and didn't return to it until much later. When I returned to it he needed it more than I did.

According to Andrews, affection is often rejected in gay life. Because of their childhood inhibitions many gays don't understand or experience affection and go through life without warmth, tenderness, or love. Andrews said that it is extremely difficult to ask someone to treat him tenderly, because it is a sign of weakness.

GOTTLIEB: You don't want to be a sissy-boy.

ANDREWS: No. Gays like me need to be macho, terribly much more so than straights. Yet sometimes I know it's good to be touched or massaged by somebody in a completely nonsexual way. I guess it's just a need to be touched and held—macho or not.

When I discussed this with Weber his reaction was considerably different. This man whose appearance epitomizes the rugged outdoorsman, avoids affection.

GOTTLIEB: I think it's a lot easier to express sexuality in a gay situation than it is to express affection—loving, kissing, hugging, tenderness. Is it very difficult?

WEBER: Very difficult.

GOTTLIEB: Where does a fellow get his affectionate needs satisfied? Needs other than sex?

WEBER: I don't think he does. I think he has to substitute friendship and companionship for sex. But I don't think the affection that exists between a man and a woman can exist between two men.

GOTTLIEB: Why not?

WEBER: Homosexuals idealize masculinity, and affection lessens the masculinity of the other person—a strange dilemma.

GOTTLIEB: You may be right—for you.

WEBER: Too much affection makes a person less masculine and more feminine, and it's a sexual turn-off, at least for me.

This must be taken in the context of Bill Weber's seeming independence. There is a certain unattainable quality that he seems to broadcast in discussing himself and his attitudes.

Somewhat later in the sessions when Andrews and I became philosophical about the whole question of sexuality and love and affection, he asked a rhetorical question about the male orgasm and came up with a startling idea.

ANDREWS: An orgasm is so defenseless. I wonder if it's not a man's most feminine moment. The freer it is, the more open it is, the more defenseless you are. Defenselessness is weakness, and weakness, to me, is feminine. How awkward it is to reveal this especially to another man—especially when you're with him to share his exquisite strength. And if his orgasm is as good as yours, he's as defenseless and weak as you; that's wild.

GOTTLIEB: There is a feminine quality to it. I think when boys have their first wet dreams, there's a loss of control like wetting their beds. I wonder if this isn't also related to impotency, both heterosexual and homosexual.

ANDREWS: The less control, the better the orgasm, right?

GOTTLIEB: Maybe women can handle it better because it's compatible with femininity, like crying or surrendering. It's part of the whole thing of being a girl. Maybe that's one of the fundamental reasons for the inherent hostility men have toward women—that they see us in a weakened or orgasmic moment.

ANDREWS: This is so true in gay life. We show our strength, we flex our muscles, all to achieve our defenseless orgasms.

GOTTLIEB: I think you're right and that answers some of my questions. I think that compulsive sexuality, gay and straight, is a defense against this defenselessness—straights with whores, gays with tricks—it's anonymous. You don't even know their names. Clinically I've seen situations where people don't even let go with their lovers.

Defenses must be lowered to enjoy the orgasm. That is why some people have stronger orgasms when they masturbate alone. Even some women share Andrews's fear of surrender and defenselessness, and that's something gays should know. To avoid this defenseless femininity many men have only compulsive sex even with their lovers.

Compulsively sexual people, especially compulsive homosexuals who like anonymous orgasms, who function mechanically, do not really function at all. But for full sexual enjoyment, every man, even the gay, must recognize his own defenseless femininity at the moment of orgasm. The man who just uses his penis as a disembodied tool or weapon will never be satisfied.

I wondered, if it is that difficult to express oneself sexually, what is it like to come out *socially* in gay society. Is it like a fraternity? Do people make things comfortable for you? Do you have people to talk to? Are you still your own man? What do you share with other gays? Again Andrews was skeptical and perhaps bitter.

GOTTLIEB: Does the young gay expect gay society to stick by him?

ANDREWS: If so, he's in for a rude shock. He's going to face more competition than acceptance. To think of it as a cohesive entity is misleading as hell. This guy has to realize whether he wants to or not—in spite of what he wants to believe and what he's been told—he is his own responsibility and he's alone.

GOTTLIEB: He has to struggle the same way as everybody else. Every person for himself, then?

ANDREWS: What you're saying is what has been my experience. You are alone.

GOTTLIEB: What about Gay Lib or any organization that claims if you join them, they'll protect you. It's a high cost but ...

ANDREWS: They can't deliver.

The opposite attitude is expressed by Jim Price. A good-looking gay is the center of attention as is a good-looking straight. Price felt more oppressed by the straight response to his good looks than by the gay one.

PRICE: The couple of relationships I had with girls started out well but just didn't end successfully. I think it was my own doing, some weakness in myself. It's not that I wasn't attracted, it was just that I wasn't strong enough for some reason. I was incapable of making the relationship work, so the alternative seemed to be to seek something outside. Being gay might not be my sexual preference, but I am much more comfortable in an atmosphere that isn't so threatening to me as an individual. I took a look into an alternative life-style that would not be so jeopardizing.

GOTTLIEB: You seem to be threatened by women.

PRICE: Huh? Well, I'm not sure I was threatened. A lot of my friends used to go up to girls in bars and at parties and pick them up. I'd always be more shy and reserved and I guess from that standpoint I felt bad.

GOTTLIEB: You mean you felt you weren't as masculine as those fellows?

PRICE: I think maybe I did feel threatened. I did feel incompetent in certain areas. I felt incompetent to communicate what I wanted, the way I wanted things to go. I had a hard time with game playing and small talk with girls.

GOTTLIEB: You feel more comfortable being gay?

PRICE: I think I feel more comfortable within myself. I think I have matured a great deal.

GOTTLIEB: You seem to have found better human relationships—both gay and straight.

PRICE: Yes. I really feel that life for me was very superficial as a straight because the people I knew closely in

1967 and 1968 were people who were occupied with sports, which was my interest too. But they were picking up and bringing home this girl or that, and even though the guys and I were good friends, the friendship was superficial. I could never understand it. They had to be with a different girl every night. I really don't have that problem now. I'm a pretty strong person, but I didn't have the assurance at that time. I guess you are right in what you said. Being gay has helped. It has given me a sense of self.

Price seems to be running from the fact that girls find him almost too attractive, too much of a beauty, and want to change or control him. Deeply embedded in his statement, however, is a basic jealousy of the girls who are getting the attention of his male friends. It reminds me of a Valentine's Day when I was twelve and my best friend was fourteen. I was shocked and hurt when he seriously delivered a valentine to a girl instead of playing basketball with me. How could he prefer a girl to me and our basketball game? For weeks I was angry with the girl and with women in general.

In gay life Jim has been one of the fortunate ones. Because of his striking appearance, he has been successful without having to resort to orgies, bars, baths, etc. People have sought *him* out, and he has sorted through them to find those who will make few demands on him or try to change him. In line with this, he has very little narcissism, and to show off publically would embarrass him. He is, in a sense, an anonymous individual, not a beautiful gay butterfly.

We see then a contrast between Andrews and Price.

Early Sex Information and Experiences

Andrews lacks the physical qualities of Price and describes himself as a person with "good muscles but an average build." In this humorous description we can understand his feeling that going into gay life has not been like joining a fraternity or being taken care of because he is beautiful.

The process of coming out or being brought out is sometimes romanticized, but it is a difficult emotional experience. What has this resulted in for Andrews, Price and Weber? One would expect Price to come out to find promiscuity. Instead, he has found love and understanding. Weber came out looking for love but instead has found promiscuity. Andrews, the oldest of the three, came out and is still looking.

2

Narcissism—The Myth and the Gay Reality

As for Narcissus, the gods punished him for having spurned Echo by making him fall in love with his own image. The soothsayer Teiresias had predicted that Narcissus would live only until the moment he saw himself. One day when he was leaning over the limpid waters of a fountain, Narcissus caught sight of his own reflection in the water. He conceived so lively a passion for this phantom that nothing could tear him away from it, and he died there of languor. He was changed into the flower which bears his name and which grows at the edge of springs. *(New Larousse Encyclopedia of Mythology)*

Some psychiatrists mistakenly interpret the concept of Narcissism to mean punishment for one's self love, rather than punishment for spurning the love of another. Yet the point of the myth is that because Narcissus did not *share* himself, his *punishment* was to fall in love with himself. Narcissism is not the cause; it is the punishment for the person who cannot be close to another! Not all beautiful people are narcissistic, and not all ugly people are immune to it. If a person cannot share himself, no matter what he looks like, he is a candidate for narcissism in any of its forms or extremes. I say extremes because a certain amount of narcissism is healthful and actually must be present in everyone. In modest quantities narcissism is necessary to a healthy ego. It saddens me that gays are so confused by narcissism and frequently feel that an immodest quantity is essential to gay success. Too many people simply do not know it is only a substitute—and perhaps even a punishment—for self-imposed loneliness.

Jim Price, magnificently muscled and handsome as he is, is not particularly narcissistic. Only reluctantly does he talk about himself. He seems irritated when his beauty is brought up and feels that narcissism has very little application to him. Indeed, heterosexual focus on his attractiveness is precisely what he was running away from when he made his homosexual choice.

Andrews is considerably more verbal about narcissism and feels there is an excessive amount of it among gays.

Bill Weber, expressing himself with his characteristic air of narcissism, has some strong ideas about it in terms of gay sexuality.

GOTTLIEB: Do you contemplate your own muscles and your own penis? Are you looking for that in somebody else?

WEBER: Yes. Or else he has to be greater than you—greater than you yourself.

Narcissism—The Myth and the Gay Reality

GOTTLIEB: What's your attitude if somebody is more attractive than you?

WEBER: Well, I think this is really a primitive idea, but the physical contact somehow makes you feel more powerful, more attractive, more self-centered. There's a tendency to feed your own narcissism. It's a little bit of a cliché, but I think the attractiveness of the other person seems to rub off.

GOTTLIEB: What do you mean by "rub off?"

WEBER: Just that. During the sex act the attractiveness of the other person becomes part of you and enhances you.

Obviously Weber doesn't know that narcissism is a punishment. Andrews realistically indicates that physical attractiveness is an important point of gay negotiability.

ANDREWS: So much, if not all is dependent upon your negotiability as a gay. To be less than perfect can be rough. Ugliness is rough; aging is rough. You *have* to be attractive.

GOTTLIEB: What about a person who is ill or deformed?

ANDREWS: He has one hell of a time.

As we talked I became very concerned about the poor guy who does not have the looks to be a popular gay. A case in point is the ordinary gay in love with an Adonis gay who needs another Adonis to turn *him* on. Most of us are average, but gay men have a hard time accepting that. Is the average-looking gay destined to be only a spectator, or can he make out? As a psychiatrist I would like to know if he does and how he does it.

Andrews seemed to have more to say about this than the other two men since he has an air of plainness that makes him inconspicuous in a crowd.

GOTTLIEB: Is gay attractiveness just skin deep?

ANDREWS: I think I have a greater chance of meeting a mate in a straight situation than in a gay one. There are more gay than straight narcissists.

GOTTLIEB: There are some rather unattractive heterosexuals who seem to get together and make very good marriages. Some attractive men marry unattractive women, and vice versa. There seems to be something for everybody.

ANDREWS: Sometimes the same thing happens with gays. There are matches that are incomprehensible from a cosmetic standpoint.

At this point I laughed nervously and did not know why.

ANDREWS: You're laughing because it really strikes home. It's absurd, yet it's meaningful. I know I'm not what I would be if I had my druthers. Within limits I can build my body, but I don't feel limited working my mind in order to change, to grow, to accomplish, and maybe to attract.

GOTTLIEB: Would you say there is a higher proportion of very attractive men who are gay?

ANDREWS: Well, here in L.A. there is, but I don't know about middle America. Some gays inherit their physical beauty and other gays have to work to develop it—good bodies and all. I didn't inherit a good body, but I've tried to enhance what I have. I think it's important to maintain yourself to answer your narcissistic need as a homosexual. Gays need exercise.

Price had something more to offer when I asked him about unattractive gays.

Narcissism—The Myth and the Gay Reality

PRICE: They have a hard time. It's harder for them unless they have other qualities, unless they have some strength inside. To a certain extent appearance for a gay is as important—if not more so—than for the straight. Of course, there are a lot of different scenes and a lot of different viewpoints. I think they really have a harder time finding happiness. With the guilt of being gay you really should have something going for you. Like the person who is not terribly attractive should become immersed in his job and all that enters into it. I think such a person has to stress personality and a sense of humor.

An unattractive gay must rely on deeper factors than his appearance and develop himself socially and professionally as much as he can. This is the situation in straight life, too, where some people have compensated for a lack of physical beauty by becoming good statesmen, artists, and scholars. In one way or another they may have made themselves more interesting than the very attractive individual who remains dull.

There is a part of narcissism that is not quite as attractive as we have described. Real self-centeredness, real narcissism, can also be involved in depression and self-hatred. Andrews, who has gone through several periods of severe depression, seems to be the most reflective about this.

ANDREWS: I've tried to find out how much I love myself, how much I hate myself, how much I simply ignore myself.

GOTTLIEB: I notice that you're referring here to "myself." These are all aspects of narcissism, yet we always think it means someone who likes to look at his own image, someone who thinks he's very attractive. We don't like to look at the self-centeredness involved in self-hatred and depression as a part of narcissism, but it is.

ANDREWS: It is not really self-hatred; it is self-disrespect.

GOTTLIEB: You know, you're the first person I've heard mention this. I would state it more in terms of self-depreciation, which is part of depression.

ANDREWS: Gay humor is filled with self-criticism and self-put-downs. Self-loathing is also frequently part of gay life.

GOTTLIEB: You mean that being depressed and not liking oneself is a condition of being gay?

ANDREWS: To some extent it is, but the gay must face it and cope with it and, hopefully, overcome it.

GOTTLIEB: This is one of the problems in psychiatry. Many psychiatrists and analysts hope that this attitude toward oneself will be so great that the patient will insist that we change him into a straight.

ANDREWS: That's a hell of an evangelical point of view.

GOTTLIEB: I agree. For the male gay a vagina is not an antidepressant.

ANDREWS: No. It certainly isn't.

GOTTLIEB: It is not narcissistic to respect and like yourself. It is narcissistic to adore yourself and also narcissistic to hate and pity yourself. There is something to be said for just learning to like yourself.

Although all people dislike themselves sometimes, this dislike often becomes exaggerated in the homosexual. When I dislike myself and become depressed, I can relieve it by indulging in some superficiality like having an extra drink or buying myself something. Most people, straight and gay, do this.

But many gays with societal and personal pressures tend

to exaggerate this normal depression by becoming bitchy and alienating their friends.

For protracted periods of time, we may have no significant people in our lives. During these periods, the gay, you, or I are subject to the most profound depression. This depression becomes more self-centered and more narcissistic the more alone we are. It is at these times—when people are so alienated, so alone, so lonely—that they take their lives. Self-imposed loneliness is the greatest enemy of the gay—or anyone.

We must keep other people around, not only to love and comfort us, but to be objects for our anger—rational or irrational. Many gays are already alienated from their families; so, if they quarrel with lovers or friends, they have no one at all. It is important to have at least one friend to talk to, and, if the depression is severe and persistent, a psychiatrist should be consulted.

Weber, an admitted exhibitionist, made a very interesting statement regarding narcissism.

WEBER: I'm sort of in-between about narcissism. I think that perhaps narcissism and homosexuality may be one and the same thing. But in my own personal experience, when I got away from narcissism, I also got away from the feeling that I'm homosexual. That's my own personal case.

Weber thinks it's inferior to be homosexual and better to identify with the norm in society. On the other hand, when one is narcissistic one is noticed in gay life, and for that reason many gays institutionalize narcissism.

A homosexual will go to great lengths to satisfy appearances. Because he himself may be personally involved in narcissistic display, he puts great stress on the quantitative—the numbers—rather than the qualitative aspects of life. Unfortunately, the man who has made many conquests is admired; the faithful, conscientious, dedicated man is unnoticed and unappreciated.

Weber feels that the quantitative measure of success he knew during the sixties is being replaced by a more qualitative view today. He feels this is due to society's improved acceptance of a gay life-style. I disagree. If there is such acceptance, I haven't seen it.

Again Weber, with his encyclopedic sexual experience revealed his efforts to maintain his own image.

GOTTLIEB: I think it's very adolescent when a straight brags about his sexual conquests and skills. There is an urgent need for him to be one of the boys, and to be one of the boys is to have many, many sexual experiences.

WEBER: That's part of an egotistic attitude. And in fact even I had an experience I told you about before, with a person in this city who was the ultimate fantasy type for a homosexual—a homosexual's dream guy. I really didn't like him, but I stayed with him for two years in absolute misery because of my own involvement, my ego involvement. I wanted the attention that came from being associated with him. I just wanted to show everybody that I could pull it off, and yet I really, really didn't like the guy. This guy was so self-centered that he provoked me into having as many orgasms as possible and yet would not let go of his. I was trying to use him to build myself up, and I think he was trying to use me to build himself up. Neither of us did anything but get involved with each other and made no plans to prepare ourselves for the future. The relationship failed.

GOTTLIEB: What do you recommend in situations like this? A person finds himself so involved in being the center of attention that he chooses somebody else who wants to be the center of attention too, and they go nowhere.

WEBER: Avoid them. It leads to absolute and utter destruction.

Weber's comments suggest that narcissism freezes a person in his past. When it is necessary for him to face reality and he actually realizes his chronological age, he is suddenly aware that he is no longer an adolescent or a young adult, but a middle-aged man. If he is constantly worried about how he appears at the present time, there is bound to be an almost one-dimensional quality to him. This makes him particularly dull and uninteresting, and sooner or later he will have to face the fact that life carries with it its tomorrows.

Andrews said the narcissist seems to pick other narcissists to project and feed upon until their relationships seem like circular affairs between two battered butterflies.

Bill Weber, whom I could hardly picture as a "battered butterfly" as he sat gesturing with his muscular arms and immensely powerful shoulders, told me how dramatic his narcissistic relationships had been. He hoped this kind of thing was over, especially since he had recently suffered a severe illness and claimed he was in the process of re-evaluating his life.

WEBER: With me the narcissism is kind of broken. When

it broke it opened up a richer life for me all over. I think very often narcissistic gay guys find almost their identical twin, in type, love object choice, etcetera. You know almost immediately because it's so obvious. First, they're so extremely good looking and there's really nothing complementary. All men are essentially built the same. They don't have the complementary thing that men and women have, the fitting together, so I think the relationship—to last—has to have something else to complement them. They cannot be alike. Otherwise it's a totally narcissistic meeting of the bodies and not of the minds, and it's got to come to an end.

GOTTLIEB: It seems to be repeated over and over again.

WEBER: Yes. It's going to be repeated. In my case, I repeated it through six very traumatic relationships. Two of them were three-year relationships which I didn't like at all.

GOTTLIEB: Each one was traumatic?

WEBER: Every one. By the sixth time I had to say the guy was a son of a bitch, I realized the other guy wasn't a son of a bitch. *I* was doing something wrong.

GOTTLIEB: But what about your own narcissistic character? How can you tolerate it over so many years?

WEBER: Well, there's absolutely nothing in it. First of all you have to be sexually compulsive. That holds it together. That's really the only thing that holds it together—sexual compulsiveness. This is true because there are no roles to divide it up when *two* people are looking for the same thing. In my case I was always supposedly the aggressor, the dominant one. The other male would usually be a passive person. In actuality, emotionally, I was really the weak one being manipulated by the other person. He was carrying out more of the narcissistic thing than I was. I would lose, so then I would go on, and on, and try to gain something without realizing who was calling the shots. I really wanted to choose another game to play.

This sounds very much like repetition compulsion, a need to go over and over material or activities in life in order to work out a fundamental problem within. In plain English, that is getting in a rut.

There was a nervous urgency about what Weber said when I pursued the subject of repetition compulsion.

GOTTLIEB: I guess you found yourself constantly seeking the most attractive people and living with each of them over a long period of years?

WEBER: That's quite true.

GOTTLIEB: What were you trying to do?

WEBER: Maybe trying to make it into a man and wife situation, but it's a real mess. It's awfully rough. In gay life it's like two mirrors reflecting against each other, reacting and recurring at the same time. It's a horrible state. I'm not saying that there can't be mating or that there isn't hope for homosexual relationships, but this kind of ... this narcissism cannot be the basis for them. Obviously they'll self destruct. I guess this is one of the reasons that gays have such a bad reputation. We tend to laugh and say we've had more marriages than Lana Turner. Then we go into our thirties, forties, and fifties repeating the same thing, each time losing our grip a bit more.

I think every homosexual has to ask himself whether the relationship he's in is really pleasant or indeed making his life miserable. There is a tendency to make your life miserable to prove a point, a narcissistic point. Relate this to the guy who is looking in the mirror. In the gyms, the

47

bars, and everywhere else, constantly looking for a change
in partners, constantly looking at himself. Why this search?
I feel it's a constant state of masturbation. It's a constant
state of about to become involved and then getting out. If a
person can honestly say no and outgrow the narcissism, and
say, "This is the person I want to be with until sixty-five,"
then maybe he has passed the narcissistic test.

GOTTLIEB: Tell me about this "constant state of
masturbation."

WEBER: When I was actually involved in homosexuality
I was also a very active masturbator. In addition I found
that after going out hustling I'd later masturbate at home.
Then I began to realize that I was extremely narcissistic. I
wouldn't release my orgasm during the thing with the
client. Later maybe I'd think about the situation and
masturbate. The most narcissistic mates I ever had usually
were masturbators. In spite of being in bed and supposedly
relating to each other physically and emotionally, they
wanted me to relate to them with my penis—somehow—
while they masturbated.

A little narcissism is a beautiful thing; a lot of it becomes
ugly. Remembering the origin of the word, I wanted to carry
the dicussion to its logical or illogical conclusion, and I
aksed Weber if his own body excited him.

WEBER: Oh sure, absolutely!

GOTTLIEB: Looking in the mirror and getting an erection
and . . .

WEBER: Masturbating. Of course. This is very common
among homosexuals. This is why they often want mirrors
while they have sex. They're looking at themselves being

caressed by another person. They're not looking at the other person.

GOTTLIEB: I've never been involved in this, but I presume my own excitation in heterosexual situations would be to watch the other person, the woman, becoming excited.

WEBER: No. The homosexual watches himself being caressed and gets excited over that. Watching themselves being adored or caressed, maybe they want to be caressed in an infantile way, and they are in love with their own bodies. But what's the next step? If you're in love with your own body, how do you make someone else love your body? That's what I think straights don't understand about the compulsive homosexual—his love for his own body. It's not enough just to masturbate in front of the mirror. The next step is to get someone to come in and masturbate on you, or they can participate and adore you while you masturbate. To carry it to its logical, nonsensical extreme, the more people you can do, the more verification you have of your own attractiveness.

GOTTLIEB: What recommendation do you have for someone who finds himself masturbating excessively in this way?

WEBER: Old age.

The conversation became more serious as we agreed that as a person grows old he must make some other adjustments. He must have other activities beyond his own self-centeredness to take his mind off aging. To amplify the point, Weber described some parties he has attended—the ones that I would call parties of desperation.

WEBER: You go to the party to see new faces, but they're all recycled ones. Year after year they keep coming back—

faces dusted off, hair recut—presenting themselves fresh to homosexual society. Many rich homosexuals often hold court to a bevy of young, attractive ones—like a Roman orgy, a pool party. Movie producers will invite two hundred of the most attractive bodies in town. To be invited to such a party is to be categorized as desirable. When you reach a certain age, you're either rich enough to throw such parties, or you're out of it. Maybe then it's better to make some kind of adjustment to being a human being rather than a narcissistic sex object. It's an indictment of the strict narcissistic approach to life.

So far I have been depressed by the very narrow range of happiness projected for the homosexual. Is the gay male someone who blooms early and has little or no future? Someone who is contaminated by the curse of narcissism?

Andrews seems to have an answer for this problem. He is not as good looking as he would like to be—a potential narcissistic curse. He treats this with humor and, on the surface, seems to be handling it adequately. His answer to my question about narcissism was, "A gay narcissist may be fun to play with, but I wouldn't want my son to marry one."

Narcissism in its extreme sense is all take and no give. If the narcissist gives you something, it is only the pleasure of his company or the pleasure of his sexuality, and often the pleasure of his moodiness. He witholds the pleasure of his person or of his character. If one is particularly attractive, it is extremely important to develop other qualities to become a whole person. Without inherent abilities or attractive qualities, one can adjust to gay life by developing into a total person and becoming something other than a compulsive machine that only attracts or is attracted to sexuality.

There is an actual curse of beauty—the Adonis narcissistic type of heterosexual or homosexual who gets attention because of his beauty. One of the problems he has to overcome is being an ornament or badge prized by others. If he attains some degree of prominence, others attribute to him extremely good taste—to him, food tastes better, he smokes better cigarettes, and he must be a good judge of wine and whiskey. Other people want to possess him and be like him. Most of the time he is expected to be more than he actually is and instilled with qualities that do not belong to him. Such an individual must learn to be his own man. A thing of beauty is *not* always a joy forever.

3

Fantasies, Orgies, Impotence, and Compulsive Sex

As a psychiatrist dealing with sexuality, one of my primary concerns is for the fantasy life of the individual: what is thought of before sexual activity and how patterns change during the sexual experience. These thought patterns, rather than actions, are the clues to sexual identification as a homosexual or heterosexual.

Some heterosexuals have homosexual fantasies, and some homosexuals have heterosexual fantasies. When it becomes too confusing to unscramble, a person can panic and it may be necessary to consult a psychiatrist.

I feel that the study of fantasy is important for another reason, one I'm more concerned with here. While fantasies are necessary for sexual activity, they can interfere with intimacy and love if one relates to the fantasy and not to the partner.

Andrews thinks some gay fantasies are so institutionalized that they become nonsexual.

ANDREWS: People who zealously burlesque fantasy—the leather queens, the uniform queens, etcetera—have hangups that become absurd and grotesque because their fantasy obliterates sex and reduces it to exaggerated symbolism.

GOTTLIEB: What you object to is wearing your fantasy on your sleeve.

ANDREWS: Right. I think it can dull sex and sometimes it's better kept secret just to keep sex exciting.

To make one's inner life known is difficult. If it can be done through some kind of structure, some kind of joint fantasy, some kind of institution such as wearing leather or chains, it is more acceptable and you are relieved at not being alone. But you cannot relate to leather and chains. You have to relate to individuals, so you may still be very much alone.

At some time in our lives most of us feel that there is something terribly abnormal about our sexual fantasies. Patients often give elaborate, guarded introductions to fantasy material. I can often state their fantasies to them before they can verbalize them. They are rather astonished by this, but my psychiatric experience indicates that there are common fantasies that can be embellished both heterosexually and homosexually. There are just so many things that humans can think and do and they usually fall into patterns.

I asked Andrews about verbalizing these fantasies.

ANDREWS: I said before that institutionalizing a fantasy

can dull sex, yet I think sharing your wants can be helpful. The point is you can be open without making a fool of yourself.

GOTTLIEB: To try to please each other is very important, but what about the fear of being rejected?

ANDREWS: You take your chances.

GOTTLIEB: Is it possible to experience fantasies with someone with whom you feel very close—someone who fulfills the needs for friendship?

ANDREWS: I don't know about other people but my greatest pleasures are with friends with whom I occasionally have sexual relations. This doesn't eliminate the quick sex, the "snack sex" kind of thing. It's just extra fun to share a fantasy with a good friend who's also a turn-on.

GOTTLIEB: It's necessary then to comingle your fantasies with the other person's?

ANDREWS: I think it may make things better sooner, but it does open you to the threat of closeness and even friendship.

GOTTLIEB: That's fascinating, "the threat of friendship."

ANDREWS: A gay premise is that you're either friends *or* lovers, and that's asinine.

Andrews's attitude toward having a full life is that one incorporates friendship, sexuality, and love into the homosexual relationship. Weber, on the other hand, rather tersely dismisses the concept of love, friendship, and sexuality being comingled. He implies that sexuality stands alone and is almost a contaminant to a friendship. A person can be either a friend or a lover, but not both.

GOTTLIEB: What if you communicate your fantasies or your feelings to the other person?

WEBER: I never do.

GOTTLIEB: Oh, I see.

WEBER: Other people have told me what their fantasies were. I kind of liked to know so that I could satisfy them better.

GOTTLIEB: Do you think it brings people close together when there's a communication of fantasies?

WEBER: That's hard to answer because there's still the separateness and the polarity. Isolation makes individuals want to come together, but there has to be a mystique of separateness in order to have the excitement of feeling. I don't know too much of what can dilute that excitement. If somebody has a very definite sexual preference or fantasy, his way of enjoying it must be communicated or else the sexual relationship has to terminate.

GOTTLIEB: If that sexual preference happens to correspond with yours, then it's exciting?

WEBER: Sure.

GOTTLIEB: If there's a reasonable correspondence of fantasy it might lead to some kind of closeness?

WEBER: It could be sexuality only.

GOTTLIEB: It has to do with sexuality only?

WEBER: Yes. It has to do with your fantasies. I don't want to get any closer than the sexuality.

There is a definite divergence of opinion between Weber and Andrews, Andrews taking the constructive attitude that one can be both friend and lover and Weber, that sexuality becomes enhanced only when there is a distance between the two people. Weber also says that friendship is always separate from sexuality. This attitude keeps him away from very close relationships and protects him in his long-term involvements.

Fantasies, Orgies, Impotence, and Compulsive Sex

All six of Weber's long-term relationships were long on sexuality and romance but short on friendship and love. Fullness *is* love and friendship; emptiness is compulsive sex and unshared fantasy.

If fantasy alone nourishes you, you become detached. Detachment leads to being jaded. Being jaded leads to being alone, even in a crowd. Maturation stops and aging accelerates.

Andrews stated that distinguishing between gay appearance and gay reality takes a long time. If you are full of fantasy, you tend to inject that fantasy into a partner. You can grossly overestimate him and become dissillusioned and bitterly angry. It becomes difficult to see the world and the people in it as they are.

Extremes in gay life where fantasies run rampant are baths and orgies.

GOTTLIEB: In both baths and orgies is there an exchange of fantasies or is it pretty much private in your experience?

ANDREWS: You mean verbal exchange?

GOTTLIEB: Yes. Do people say what they are feeling?

ANDREWS: I dropped out of the orgy scene years ago because I couldn't get it on. I was so uptight about it I literally couldn't get turned on. Try as I could, the flashing whiff of exhausted poppers and spent sex made it impossible.

GOTTLIEB: Do gays think poppers—amyl nitrite—really intensify orgasms?

ANDREWS: Amyl Semple McNitrite, high priestess of sex. Part of straight life too, David. Maybe it helps some people share something during orgies. It doesn't help me because gay orgies are so anonymous they're masturbatory. They can be so absurd some people actually giggle.

GOTTLIEB: Giggling equals impotence.

ANDREWS: Right. And impotence is bad manners.

GOTTLIEB: Same with straights.

ANDREWS: The point is, don't break the orgy mood.

GOTTLIEB: That's your opinion. What about others?

ANDREWS: I really don't know. There are some people who feel they have really triumphed if they suck a mile of cock a night. They may not have orgasms doing it. Now that to me is fantasy.

GOTTLIEB: And what I detect is an absence of romance.

There are no standard sexual practices among gays, but there is considerable variation. There are questions of passivity versus aggressivity, dependence versus independence, and dominance versus submission. The passive sexual partner in a gay relationship can in actual fact be the aggressor. The whole area is extremely confused by the desire of straight society and psychiatrists to imprint on gay life certain kinds of stereotyped behavior.

Gay men, like straight men, are concerned with masculinity. Many gay and straight men won't admit they like to be on the bottom sexually, no matter how much they enjoy it. Both gays and straights talk freely in therapy and to each other about their aggressive tendencies, but both are extremely reluctant to talk about their passive fantasies.

If they do admit to passivity, they admit to being feminine. This fear of femininity inhibits exchange of fantasies. Somehow it is okay to say they want to be assertive and penetrate, but it's not okay to say, "I want to *be* penetrated."

Because of this inhibition, many gays do not know how to

posture themselves with their lovers. The most common complaint among my straight patients is that they would like their wives to be more aggressive. When I confront these men with the fact that theirs is a feminine desire, they are frightened and shocked. Some of them would rather their wives be sexually dominant, but they are so ashamed they settle for simply being henpecked. There is no one as obvious as the henpecked stud.

The three men with whom I talked evinced a kind of naiveté about what other people do. They felt themselves estranged from homosexuality in its entirety, and they felt that they represented a small segment of the total homosexual population.

As a straight psychiatrist, I can speak for straight sexuality with more authority. It is simpler, and the roles are delineated. The new sexual therapies are successful since they focus primarily on making the individual relax in his or her particular role. For gays, sexual therapy is extremely difficult because gays compete over particular roles that are not as easily delineated.

Maybe this explains the popularity of gay baths and orgies. There one can relax and remain anonymous.

Andrews suggested that the homosexual may be in fact a *homosocial* individual upon whom nature imposes sexuality. An individual chooses a member of his own sex as a sexual object, but his primary concern is to choose someone as a *social* object. Then sexuality comes in, not necessarily as a contaminant, but as a physical necessity. In other words, all men are attracted to each other socially and must find a way of discharging their sexual impulses, too. The manner of discharging these sexual impulses distinguishes gays from straights. If you do not recognize your *homoso-*

cial needs, you can become involved in compulsive, repetitive, ungratifying sexuality.

Weber, the "sexual encyclopedia," illustrates this most clearly.

GOTTLIEB: Could you elaborate on compulsive sex?

WEBER: When I was very compulsively sexual it seemed like the more danger involved, the more exciting it was. The furtiveness of doing something on the beach at night or in the backseat of a car was far more exciting than doing it in a private place. I don't know what comes first, that it's exciting because it's secretive, or that it's secretive and then becomes exciting. There are also people who like to be witnesses.

GOTTLIEB: What do you mean?

WEBER: I mean I used to get my kicks by performing while other people watched. Now I would only get involved with someone I cared enough about to do it privately.

GOTTLIEB: You distance yourself and decrease the intimacy by having sex with other people watching.

WEBER: Yes. There's no special kind of relationship because it's a communal kind of thing.

GOTTLIEB: It kind of reinforces the idea of wanting to be independent. I don't know how satisfying that is over the long haul.

WEBER: Whenever I was on that trip I had to have sex quite frequently.

GOTTLIEB: It would seem that the more frequent the need for sex, the less the satisfaction.

WEBER: The more anonymous, the more furtive, the more secretive the experience, the more compulsive the need to repeat it and the less the satisfaction. The more frequently I picked up people on the street or on the beach, the less satisfying it was.

GOTTLIEB: But usually for a man and woman during sexual experience there's a feeling of pleasant fatigue after the sexual act—a kind of relief or relaxation.

WEBER: With this other kind of sex, it was just the opposite. I was alerted; I was not relaxed. As soon as I completed the sexual act I wanted to leave, to wash, immediately. I would not be relaxed; I would be nervous. I wanted to put as much distance between myself and that person as possible.

GOTTLIEB: That's a universal situation. I don't know if you're aware of it, but in a heterosexual situation as well as in a homosexual one with a trick, there is a desire to get away from the sexual act itself, to leave the situation, not to stay overnight. So if you do share your fantasies with the person and you get close to him, maybe there's a chance that you can stay with that individual and relax.

WEBER: No, I don't think so. If it's compulsive sex—and it would have to be my fantasy type—then it would be a physical thing only. It would be a "sperm of the moment" meeting—a trick at the beach or something, and then goodbye, because it was based on physical sex fantasy and not upon getting to know and like the person. I think my habits are beginning to change now.

Compulsive, furtive sex becomes a major part of his life when a gay feels he has no other choice. Many straights criticize this "typical" behavior of gays. They believe that gays are sexual athletes who will contaminate all of society by spreading their peculiar physical and emotional disease. They are modern-day lepers.

Any person whose pattern is compulsive sexuality may have lovers, but it is doubtful that he has love. To such an individual, the concept of sexuality is completely unrelated to the concept of love.

Fusing love and sex is a necessity, not only for personal happiness, but for the preservation of civilization—across the board, for gays and straights alike. Certainly sexuality is enjoyable by itself, but such recreational sex is not the be-all and end-all of life. Straights may have difficulty defining love, but gays have even more difficulty. Finding love becomes more of a challenge for gays than for straights; so they seem to settle for high sexuality and fleeting lovers.

For a long time, I thought gays were universally potent and that impotence was restricted to heterosexuals. I was somewhat hostile toward homosexuals and probably unconsciously envied them because they always seemed able to perform. I find that this is absolutely not the case, and there may actually be a higher incidence of impotency in gay life.

Andrews indicated his preoccupation with potency.

ANDREWS: Why don't you tell me what happens to a person's life during his thirties and forties? How long can a person maintain an erection? The excitation levels—when do they perceptibly diminish and how? What is there to expect out of male sex life?

GOTTLIEB: What is there to expect?

ANDREWS: Yes, straight or gay.

GOTTLIEB: I'll have to give you an overview of what I've seen in patients. I think that particularly in the teens and through age thirty there is a fairly active sexual drive. My guess is that heterosexual activity occurs about three or four times a week.

ANDREWS: That's all?

GOTTLIEB: This is what I've heard. When people first get married they usually have much more sexual activity but it tapers off.

ANDREWS: What about the ability to be stimulated, the quality of the stimulation? I'm awfully confused on this point.

GOTTLIEB: I would say that you're not talking about frequency in terms of a qualitative experience. If you're not forcing the issue, a person can perform in a qualitative way until he's forty-five as well as he did when he was twenty or twenty-five.

ANDREWS: What about loss of erection? Nonerection? Nonejaculation? You turn sour, what happens? Does that happen frequently?

GOTTLIEB: Sure.

ANDREWS: Does it happen frequently in a young person?

GOTTLIEB: Probably not as frequently.

ANDREWS: But it does happen?

GOTTLIEB: I think so. In terms of gay sexuality there's a lot of excitation, a lot of sexual stimulation that comes from the novelty of the situation early on. Then, as a person gets older, it's harder for him to get excited.

ANDREWS: What about a gay guy who's in his thirties or forties? Do you think he should fear for his potency or the loss of it?

GOTTLIEB: I don't see any reason why. You may not be able to have sex as frequently but the quality should improve with age. Quality goes up and quantity may go down. Many straights and gays try to recapture something that existed earlier in their lives. They are almost competing with their images of themselves as youngsters. But it doesn't work and inevitably their sexual frequency falls off. For those who are constantly preoccupied with their sexual image, it can fall off suddenly and frighteningly.

Andrews stated that there is an amazing amount of impotency among gays—far more than they will admit, perhaps more among gays than among straights.

ANDREWS: I asked you some questions earlier about what a male can expect out of life, because I know that a lot of people are terribly unhappy and doubt their own sexual ability.

GOTTLIEB: Let me point out that as a straight looking at gay society, I am kind of amazed to hear that there is such a degree of impotence there. Almost by definition we think of gay ...

ANDREWS: Supersexuality.

Very rarely does a homosexual come into the office complaining about impotence, yet this is a common complaint of a male heterosexual patient. Perhaps an impotent gay is so self-conscious he would not seek medical or psychiatric aid. It is a double put-down to be both gay and impotent.

Weber, who seemed to be the epitome of potency, surprised me when I asked him about it.

GOTTLIEB: Has potency ever been a problem for you?
WEBER: It is a big problem for me.
GOTTLIEB: I thought that gays could walk around with a

perpetual hard-on, but maybe that's a myth. A lot of straights envy this in the gay.

WEBER: If they walk around with a big hard-on most of the time, sooner or later they're going to walk around with it hanging limp for many months too. I think gays have as many impotency problems as straights have. It can follow a disastrous sexual relationship. It can follow being used as a dildo, sexually, to a point where you can't get it up because it's too dehumanized. If you get depressed, and gays get very depressed, extremely so, they can be hypersexual to fight the depression. Or, if they really have a good case of depression, they can be impotent. Your ego enters into it too. If you see yourself as a sexual hotshot and you can't get it up, that makes for a period of impotency, and it can throw you into a period of depression.

There's another phenomenon that also occurs. You can idealize somebody for a long period of time, and when you get into bed with him find yourself impotent. You get what you think is your ultimate partner, and this can happen.

GOTTLIEB: You are then concentrating on performance.

WEBER: That's right.

GOTTLIEB: If a person concentrates on performance, his ability to perform sexually will diminish considerably.

Does the gay burn out sexually if he does not build up strong love and friendship relationships where he is comfortable in expressing his sexuality? If he is constantly treating himself as a compulsively oriented sexual object, he will not be able to maintain his potency.

To both gay and straight, potency is the essence of masculinity. One sure way to decrease potency is to decrease affection and love outlets. If one is oriented to performance only, he may not be able to perform.

The concept of performing connotes a staged situation, a depersonalization of sexuality—acting without feeling. Some people can function only when sex is depersonalized. However, this cannot last for an extended period of time. Sooner or later, depersonalized sex will fail to the point of almost complete impotency.

There is a considerable amount of inhibition of sexuality and feeling among male homosexuals. Andrews seems to agree.

GOTTLIEB: Would you say that gays can sometimes be very inhibited sexually?

ANDREWS: Yes.

GOTTLIEB: That'll surprise a lot of straights.

ANDREWS: We can appear bright and charming and sexual but be quite the opposite when the chips—and the pants—are down. We're pictured as sexual sophisticates but I think few of us are. We're not as sexually creative as the world believes.

GOTTLIEB: But shouldn't you be?

ANDREWS: Of course. But even gays substitute playacting for creativity much of the time.

GOTTLIEB: But if you're going to have sex, then do it and have fun.

ANDREWS: Agreed. If it were only that simple, David, but poor performance—failure—can take the fun out of it.

GOTTLIEB: Yes.

ANDREWS: Sexual failure can be disastrous, especially to gays.

GOTTLIEB: It is true that failure can be disastrous to gays, just as it can be disastrous to straights, but there's a point where gays won't even talk about it.

ANDREWS: That's what I'm saying. We're ashamed of it. We want to present outselves as superstuds.

GOTTLIEB: Maybe that's why some of my gay patients are competitive with me—because I'm the straight male.

ANDREWS: They compare you as a straight male to themselves as gay males and they think gay males are better than straight males, right?

GOTTLIEB: Yes. They tend to feel superior. When people have a feeling that they're not up to what society wants, they feel that what they *are* is better than society.

When we feel a discrepancy between our views and attitudes and another group's attitudes, hostility, friction, fear—primarily fear—build up. There is a kind of interface between gays and straights in which I find myself trying to bring the material on orgies, sexual activities, and impotency together. I find all of my old platitudes falling short of the mark. All of the attitudes that I have developed in psychiatric practice seem to leave me. In other words, I am left in the position of the doctor who cannot cure the patient, but must sit, watch, and wonder.

4

Variations on a Theme— S&M, B&D, and Other Aberrations

There are certain distortions of sexuality that I would label abnormal wherever they occur. Among these are violence, sado-masochism, bondage and discipline. They exist in both gays and straights, but unfortunately they have become more indentified with gay life.

Andrews wanted to dispel some of the unreasonable fears the heterosexual has of the gay. More and more of these fears appear daily in the press. One of these is the misconception that gays will spread their "evil" sexual ways to innocent young men. According to Andrews, gays cannot proselytize because a real heterosexual cannot be seduced. He simply cannot get it up. However, a homosexual can be seduced by a heterosexual and frequently is—sometimes only to be beaten in order to satisfy the sadistic needs of the straight seducer.

Andrews defines this "rough trade" as any trick who beats

up his sexual partner and gets pleasure from doing so. We have all heard of beatings and killings of gays by straights, and often the straights get off free even though their involvement and actions are premeditated.

Andrews feels that "rough-trade" characters are violent sexual bigots who get into such a hang-up about sexuality and their sexual identification that they become wild. They do not like what they are doing or the person with whom they are doing it, and they make that person the victim of their rage. Primarily, though, they hate themselves, and violence is an externalization of their self-hate. Unaccountably, I was embarrassed to ask Andrews about homosexual violence.

GOTTLIEB: What do you think about the possibility of rape occurring between homosexuals?

ANDREWS: Actual rape—not likely—but "stage rape"with everyone a willing actor—yes. It can be degrading and gay degradation is quite fashionable today.

GOTTLIEB: With such people there's a fusion of a tremendous hostile aggression and sexuality. I've really not quite understood the type of person who gets involved with degradation, either heterosexual or homosexual. Rape always includes degradation. I wonder how much latent homosexuality is present in a heterosexual rapist.

ANDREWS: I don't know. A further question is how much latent homosexuality exists in anyone.

GOTTLIEB: I think "latent homosexuality" has become a psychiatric put-down—a psychiatric degradation. It's an overused concept, and I don't know what it means. At one time it was a definitive term. You were "latently homosexual" only if you were overly concerned with proving your masculinity—a Don Juan character. Like so many other psychiatric concepts, it has taken on so many meanings that now it has none.

Because a gay is a pariah in society, any time we find something undesirable or ugly we attribute it to him. Malevolence runs rampant in the human being; so we all carry a list of people and things to blame for our own shortcomings. One of the greatest antidepressants in the world is to have a population of gays to hate and fear. Then we do not have to get angry with ourselves. At least in modern times gays, more than any other group, bear the brunt of society's prejudice. The worst thing to call a guy is "fag."

Another question came up: Is there more violence in the homosexual than in the heterosexual population?

Andrews has known many gays who have been bruised and beaten in sexual situations. He concluded unhappily that in homosexuality, as in any subcultural group, there is a great potential for violence. A person in a subcultural group may feel less control during a passionate interchange.

GOTTLIEB: Why do you feel that self-control is different among homosexuals?

ANDREWS: Because a respectable person is supposed to have self-control. If a person lacks self-respect—and many gays do—he lacks respect for and from others. He might be more apt to say, "Screw it. I'm going to get what I want come hell or high water," and thus asks for violence.

GOTTLIEB: I think I begin to understand what you mean.

ANDREWS: Without self-respect you are vulnerable. There's more of a hair trigger.

71

The Gay Tapes

GOTTLIEB: You'd have a greater potential for violence?

ANDREWS: I guess so if you hate yourself more than you love yourself.

Andrews obviously feels the cause of violence goes beyond a poor self-image to outright self-hatred. He feels a gay must be extremely careful if his lover or trick seems to have conflict in accepting himself and what he is doing sexually. In other words, if a person has not accepted himself as gay and has questions about his own sexuality, he then perceives his partner as being gay and wishes to destroy that part of himself that is gay—that part of himself that he condemns and toward which he feels very hostile.

The gay may be involved in his lover's panic in an unfortunate way; that is, the aggression may be turned on the partner rather than on himself. It is best in social and sexual situations to associate with somebody who feels comfortable at being himself. It is discomfort with making the choice that leads to conflict and volatility—the essence of destructive behavior.

Andrews pointed out the other kinds of expressions of aggression from volatile persons. Other than direct physical aggression, such people can blackmail their lovers emotionally.

GOTTLIEB: What do you mean by emotional blackmail?

ANDREWS: Well, for example, a lover threatens suicide; that's a great way to make you give him what he wants.

GOTTLIEB: Are there any other forms of emotional blackmail that you can think of?

ANDREWS: You've helped build your profession cataloging them. I think extreme possessiveness is emotional blackmail.

GOTTLIEB: Yes.

ANDREWS: Permissive possessiveness is another form. You permit your partner to stray, for example. That makes him guilty and puts him in debt to you.

GOTTLIEB: Any others?

ANDREWS: Literal blackmail can keep a lover in line.

GOTTLIEB: That happens frequently?

ANDREWS: I doubt it.

Weber also had some feelings about gay self-acceptance.

GOTTLIEB: Do you think there is such a thing as normal homosexuality? Should the concept of homosexuality as a disease be thrown out of psychiatric nomenclature?

WEBER: That's an interesting concept really. I never thought about it. I guess it would be accepting oneself as being homosexual and also accepting a life-style and not apologizing for it. Self-acceptance. It's obviously not accepted at the present time legally or socially, so even now we can only begin to discuss it. It really is hard to look upon it as an acceptable kind of activity.

My question about considering homosexuality a normal variant surprised Weber. It is really like walking through life with a chip on your shoulder. Sometimes people with chips on their shoulders are reluctant to give them up. They enjoy them. They do not want acceptance because it takes away some of their *raison d'être*.

People do not become homosexuals because they want to be outcasts, but once they are pariahs, they need to cling to that as a reason for being. They are like the liberal patient I once saw who was depressed when Kennedy was elected President because he had nothing more to complain about.

The Gay Tapes

In addition to the more obvious expressions of violence and hostility, there are symbolic activities that occur in sexuality. Sado-masochism, or S&M, and bondage and discipline (B&D), occur both heterosexually and homosexually. Underground papers and some gay journals have classified ads for S&M, B&D, and other more far-out sexual activities.

Andrews felt that people who get involved in these activities are role playing. There may be some people who are sincerely interested devotees of sadism and masochism, bondage and discipline, but the other people seem to be playing roles. To him it's basically phony. These people are only advertising their own insecurity. It is too obvious. They protest too much.

Andrews said that a lot of sexuality—and particularly gay sexuality—is an intense acting-out of fantasies. It quickly loses its credibility to the participants, and the spontaneity of sexual interaction is lost, particularly when it is programmed through one of these deviant forms.

GOTTLIEB: I'd like to talk about the chains and harnesses.

ANDREWS: Then talk about them with someone else.

GOTTLIEB: Come on, Andy.

ANDREWS: Hardware is hardware. It's the meaning I abhor. If I accept it, it reduces me—because I'm gay—to nothing.

I tried to make a case for a little bit of sado-masochism and a little bit of B&D sexual activity as maybe a slight variation. Although Andrews would accept a little S&M as play, he would not accept B&D or anything beyond. He insisted B&D is destructive and reinforces the childhood idea that sex and the people involved are evil.

S&M, B&D, and Other Aberrations

GOTTLIEB: Psychoanalytically we have studied sado-masochism, B&D, and other kinds of aberrations. A person indulging in them is really trying to establish a relationship with a primary love object, most often the mother, but sometimes the father. It's very cleverly disguised through the S&M and B&D activities. Maybe some kind of forbidden, incestuous pleasure is what the individual really wants. These activities are more common among men than among women, or at least men talk about them much more. What I am trying to say is that some of this activity is part of all of us as human beings, and we must make some allowances and accept it. It exists unconsciously in all of us.

ANDREWS: Okay, but you're placing it in a different perspective then.

GOTTLIEB: Yes. That's what I'm trying to do here.

ANDREWS: S&M as a game, yes, but as a way of life, no. It so easily escalates to the depths of degradation.

Andrews feels much more danger in these aberrations than I do. Because of his experience, because of who he is, because of his feelings internal and external, and because of his attitudes toward life and the fact that he himself is gay, I have to defer to his opinion.

The problem is that because homosexuality is not really sanctioned, there is a greater tendency to go overboard and stereotype oneself in some kind of sexual aberration. Homosexuality is an exaggeration. As Andrews says, "Homosexuals are like everybody else, only more so."

When he sees activities that might be interesting or fun the gay has a tendency to involve himself without good judgment. With these activities, he becomes stereotyped and therefore does himself and his brother homosexuals a great deal of harm. What he momentarily ignores are his own long-term interests, his own needs for love in order to combat loneliness and separation from the rest of society. What Andrews is actually saying is that you must be your own man.

Weber has contrasting observations about how people use S&M and B&D to *deny* their homosexuality. It is particularly true of hustlers or those who participate in someone else's fantasies for money.

GOTTLIEB: What do you think of S&M and B&D?

WEBER: I've had no personal experience, but I think that's kind of a splinter group or subculture within the gay group.

GOTTLIEB: Do you have any feelings about this sort of thing?

WEBER: I suppose it's a good way to depersonalize sexuality. It formalizes the act. It requires costuming and it depersonalizes it. You don't relate to any person. It becomes kind of attractive to older gays because it's another way to make themselves more exciting. Black leather can cover a lot of varicosities.

GOTTLIEB: How he's dressed can literally become a cover for his flaws.

WEBER: Exotic outfits involve feeling a need to turn people on. I'll tell you something. I was a hustler myself. Most of the clients were masochistic and they expected some kind of cute role and I affected the role. There was practically no physical involvement for me. I'd be the stud; they'd usually have the costume: cowboy hats and boots or leather. I'd push them around and they'd masturbate and I'd take thirty dollars and leave.

I'd sometimes do a couple of calls in a night. Nobody knew about it and I didn't have to do anything. I thought it repulsive physically because they always accepted the fact that I was the dominant one, or they'd masturbate while I talked tough or whatever. Then I got a call that really turned me off. He wanted me to participate in his sexual problems, sexual aberrations.

GOTTLIEB: Why were you doing that as a sideline?

WEBER: I didn't figure I was going to retire on it. I was just doing it for the money, really. Among the hustlers we all knew each other, most of us. We compared notes and referred clients to one another if they didn't want to see the same hustler three or four times. I got to know some of these guys. They really were hung up on the idea of somebody's wanting them, paying for them. They needed these people more, really, than the people needed them, but they wouldn't admit it. Interestingly, getting involved in this kind of thing is a good way to deny your homosexuality. Most hustlers claim that they're not gay, and I thought that too—that I did it only for the money. But it was a chance of expressing homosexuality under the guise of not really being homosexual. I got all the best of the situations: money, attention, and excitement.

Weber found it very appealing for a period of time until he began to realize what he was doing. In spite of all the self-centered, narcissistic aspects of being a hustler, there was always the threat of running into someone he knew. He felt he could not keep up the charade, the swagger, the two phones, indefinitely; so he gave it up.

He did agree that gays get rather cynical about life and probably develop a jaded attitude early on. Most gays

77

become brittle, superficial, and mean. It makes them unpleasant, and the whole situation is difficult to cope with if you are a member of that society.

Weber is not as uptight as Andrews regarding sexuality. He has been more of a doer and less of a thinker. Recently, after a severe illness, he started reflecting on his past life. He concluded that if you are oriented toward doing things without thinking, there may be more excitement in some of the aberrant sexual activities. If you reflect on the total picture of gay life and the total impact of what you are doing, it is best to refrain from outlandish sexual activities.

Andrews's attitude has a defensive and uptight quality. He tends to be rigid in his condemnation of those who do things differently from how he does them.

The question for both straights and gays is: Can you become successfully involved with another person who is heavily into B&D, S&M, or other aberrations? Is he going to be sadistic toward you in a business arrangement? Will he be masochistic in a social situation so that you find *yourself* becoming sadistic? In other words, does his deviation spill into other areas of his life or is it self-contained?

I tell patients that some of their behavior brings out the worst in their partners. If you degrade yourself, the nicest person in the world has one of two choices: to go along with the degradation or leave. A passive, masochistic person can bring out the aggressive, sadistic beast in any other person. An aggressive, sadistic, castrating person can drive any other to a posture of emasculation or rage.

Remember that being a "naughty" or "dirty" boy or girl becomes a sexual turn-on for many. An extension of this is some kind of restriction or punishment that also becomes sexualized. The sexual need for punishment can reach its peak in homosexuality. A person may end up liking the punishment or perversion but not liking himself.

This doesn't mean that some fantasies and activities involving B&D, S&M, voyeurism, and exhibitionism should not be part of everyone's sexual arsenal. We should be able to participate in these things to titillate ourselves sexually, but it absolutely must be moderate and rational.

A couple, gay or straight, who have sex only in the dark or partially clothed, miss some of the fun and excitement of sex. They are not inventive. Inventiveness comes from tapping our "aberrant" resources. When the "aberrant" resources become the primary thing, however, something is wrong.

If a person does not allow himself a healthy outlet for these colorful fantasies with a loved one, he might end up doing someone or being done furtively in a men's room.

If he becomes totally immersed in any of these offshoots of sexuality and does not vary his approach to life, he probably has little involvement with anyone on an intimate, long-term basis. At this point he might look at himself and ask, "What the hell am I doing? Do I want to spend the rest of my life doing this?"

5

Bitch Queens,
Destructiveness,
Superficiality and Nellies

Andrews, sometimes sensitive, sometimes defensive, has had his share of the verbal back-stabbing and bitchiness that mark gay life. I asked him about this and the people who perpetrate it—the bitch queens.

Bitchiness exists in us all. My concern is whether or not its extreme form is devastating to the gay. If so, how can he handle it?

GOTTLIEB: I'm not so concerned about a direct attack. We've talked about a very biting sense of humor being predominant among gays. What I'm referring to here is the behind-the-back stabbing, whispering about a guy, what he's been doing, with whom he's been tricking. For example, a couple of gays are having a hot romance, and somebody who is jealous spreads rumors that one or both are tricking on the side. That gets back, fourth or fifth hand, in a way that is destructive to the relationship.

ANDREWS: It may not destroy it, but it sure can hurt it.

GOTTLIEB: I think a comparable situation may exist in small towns where back-fence gossip can be extremely destructive. I certainly am not denying that bitchiness exists across-the-board. But is it something that's exaggerated with the gay? Gays label it "bitch queen." I can't think of any special straight label for the same thing. Unfortunately, it's a label that is applied to straight women, not men, yet men do it just as much.

ANDREWS: Bitching means constantly griping. Everybody does that. Bitchiness, though, is a consistently destructive way of behaving. It's how a bitch queen operates and how he gets the attention he wants—by destroying or annihilating, verbally or otherwise, another person. He can be destructive just by a look or a gesture as well as by a sarcastic or cynical remark. It sure gets attention, and gays love attention.

GOTTLIEB: A straight man can bitch, in the sense of complaining, too, without losing his masculinity. But he does become less masculine if his bitching becomes his primary way of behaving. In other words, if bitchiness becomes one of his character traits. The bitch queen is considered feminine, but women aren't really as arch, satirical, or cynical as the bitch queen. He exaggerates femininity so much that he becomes almost a third sex, not really masculine, not really feminine, but *his* masculine interpretation of femininity. It's bad acting.

ANDREWS: I think you're describing a rusted-out condition that could use your kind of help. As a psychiatrist, do you agree?

GOTTLIEB: I'm not sure. Go on.

Bitch Queens, Destructiveness, Superficiality and Nellies

ANDREWS: I think gays tend to be more destructive than straights. By building up a situation and then destroying it—playfully, wantonly—we can be destructive with matters that are important to other people, even with matters that are important to ourselves. It's incredibly nihilistic.

GOTTLIEB: So many gays I have seen yearn for relationships they can't achieve.

ANDREWS: Right. Gays are drifters.

GOTTLIEB: A drifter in an impossible search for something to hang on to is certainly going to be bitter. Bitchiness doesn't exist without bitterness.

The gay places no premium on fidelity; so his relationships seem to be in flux. Given twenty or thirty people who are gay contrasted to the same number of straights, the chances of gays' changing partners is far greater. By that token, however, it seems that gays seem to leave their romantic flanks open to attack more than straights.

ANDREWS: A gay relationship is condemned and gays know and feel this. Again, I have to remark, we're a subculture, which is all the more reason to be cynical, sardonic, faithless, and bitchy.

GOTTLIEB: *You* seem rather bitter.

ANDREWS: Yes, I'm bitter about having to be bitter and angry about the oversensitized quality of gay life.

GOTTLIEB: What do you mean by oversensitized?

ANDREWS: I mean the feeling that I'm gay first and everything else is secondary. I want to be *me* first! Everything else and gay—second!

Andrews went on to describe the gay bitches with whom he had had contact. They play in a sandbox of trivia and

83

float through time without "expanding enough to fill out the stretch marks of age." I pointed out that he was describing self-centered people who are bitchy because they have to feel something to remind them that they're alive—even if it is only bitterness. This kind of reminder is an attention getter.

Some people, like magnets, attract chaotic situations to themselves. They deliberately meddle in situations so that they can become hysterical and bitchy and overreact. They thrive on this kind of food for thought and action.

Andrews agreed that things just seem to happen to some people. They always seem to be at the site of an accident or fire, figuratively and literally. Often they themselves cause the difficulty.

Andrews added that the real bitch can cause chaos by the turn of a phrase, a flippant remark, or verbal stabbing.

ANDREWS: Help me understand something. Is it the *result* of the bitchy act or simply *doing* something bitchy that satisfies the bitch queen?

GOTTLIEB: I think both. Bitchiness is a hostile aggressive attempt to create tragedy. We all have an appetite for tragedy. If it can't be satisfied vicariously we may create tragedy to feed that appetite. I repeat, bitchiness is a combination of aggression and hostility that is very hard for the recipient to handle and for the bitch queen to control.

Andrews has been the victim of bitchiness, especially when he was deeply in love some years ago. Some people delighted in his unsuccessful involvement and hurt him by deliberately telling him that his lover was running around with someone—that he was a fool. He admits he was a fool for pitying himself as much as he did. The bitch queens succeeded in reducing Andrews to a self-pitying shell of a man. Andrews says, and I agree, that acts of bitchiness by themselves can be ignored and not hurt you, but when you acknowledge them, the result is self-pity and that is the most devastating and destructive condition of all. It is one that only you can control. You can let bitchiness roll off your back like water off a duck's, or you can drown in it.

GOTTLIEB: How do you recommend handling bitchiness directed toward you?

ANDREWS: You can't ignore it. Some of it may be accurate but you can control how much of it affects you.

Price seems to be an individual only remotely involved in a bitchy attitude toward people. He feels that a bitch queen is somebody who is terribly unhappy.

PRICE: He's the kind of guy who's really unhappy with himself, and maybe he's drawing attention to himself. It's a way of getting attention he can't get by just being normal, just an everyday person.

GOTTLIEB: You feel that there is a certain amount of self-centeredness expressed by being a bitch queen? A lot of people who are real bitches are invited to a lot of parties.

PRICE: Well, they're very entertaining.

GOTTLIEB: They're sort of the gossip columnists of the gay society, people who are expert at putting others down.

PRICE: I feel that these people are constantly trying to upstage. They're constantly drawing attention to themselves.

Of the three, Weber has had more direct experience with bitchiness and bitch queens.

GOTTLIEB: What do you think about the bitch queen?

WEBER: That's camp. It's a fine line. It starts with camp humor that can turn into bitchiness. There's the kind of person who puts others down in such a clever way that it's appreciated. It may be done in jest, but it's aimed right at the heart.... No, not at the heart, right at the throat.

GOTTLIEB: Is "camp" one extreme of just being funny?

WEBER: Carried too far it becomes like the play, *Who's Afraid of Virginia Woolf?* The game becomes reality and you wonder if the funny remarks are meant to hurt or if they're for humor only. It can escalate and someone can get hurt, so I guess it's just a dangerous game and people shouldn't play it.

GOTTLIEB: Do you think that every gay is potentially a bitch queen?

WEBER: No, but I think a bitch is kind of a fun, predictable, amusing sort of person.

GOTTLIEB: Then what is a bitch? What does he do?

WEBER: A real bitch is hard to describe. But last night I had a couple in my house. For example, he looks over the food, then goes straight to the refrigerator to look for the one item that is missing, in this case, the white wine.

GOTTLIEB: He's constantly putting you down.

WEBER: Yes. A bitch will say, "Your hair looks marvelous," when you just got out of the shower and haven't bothered drying it. That's really at a minor level. There are a lot of bitch queens around. I don't take them too seriously. The open bitch queen is safe.

GOTTLIEB: What do you mean?

WEBER: Well, the one who is kind of hidden and doesn't really come out or isn't labeled as a bitch queen, might be a latent bitch queen. Certain gays who are known as bitch queens have a big following. They are witty with acid humor—like Alice Longworth, a bitch in her own way.

GOTTLIEB: Do gays do this more than straights?

WEBER: Yes.

GOTTLIEB: Why do you think there is so much bitchiness?

WEBER: I think some of it may be a verbalization of sexual frustration. It's aggression. For example, gays are going to a social gathering. It's not an orgy, no sex is involved, but there is sexual attraction. There's kind of an unwritten social code that they can't touch or be verbally seductive with each other. This happens very commonly. So a verbal aggressiveness can be created, a bitchiness, and as time goes by the person becomes more and more bitchy.

GOTTLIEB: You mean the fellow gets his rocks off verbally? Do you think that a bitch queen should change, or can change?

WEBER: Maybe he enjoys being a bitch. Most of the bitches I know are very popular. They give parties or are invited to parties just because they are bitchy. Bitchiness is the kind of commodity that they can use to bring attention to themselves.

GOTTLIEB: Like a gossip columnist?

WEBER: It's part of gay life. If you can't dish it back then you'd better evaluate the kind of friends and parties you want. At big parties there's always a bitch queen. Often a bitch queen will single out a shy but attractive person as a target.

GOTTLIEB: What's in it for someone who is a superbitch?

WEBER: They're sexually frustrated and want to reinforce themselves with their peers.

GOTTLIEB: Would such an individual come to the psychiatrist to change?

The Gay Tapes

WEBER: They're so clever and have so much to bitch about that they haven't time for analysis or psychiatry. I think they're probably using the world as a psychiatrist. They're vocalizing their hostilities in a clever way. It's their outlet for pent-up feelings. Dishing isn't necessarily bad, and being a bitch is really the lesser of several evils.

Much of what has been said needs little psychiatric clarification. The feelings and ideas are straightforward. Essentially we are talking about one small part of aggression: hostility as bitchiness, self-centeredness, and general troublemaking. We all do this some of the time, but male gays do more of it more of the time.

It is a truism that such behavior does not endear you to your fellow man, although there are certain circumstances when it is humorous. Some people who have developed a thick-skinned attitude are really entertained by the bitch queen. Presumably, however, both gays and straights want to be loved, so why does a person attract attention to himself by nasty behavior?

Being bitchy or self-centered can be equated with being superficial or shallow. A very superficial personality can not be intimate emotionally. A bitchy person does not want to be close. At least at an unconscious level, he pushes people away because closeness creates vulnerability. Vulnerability is terrifying to many people and perhaps especially to gays.

Aggression is a human instinct that can be creative as well as hostile and destructive. To be destructive there must be something to destroy—a victim. Part of the adaptation to any group is to know the vehicles of expression of anger and hostile aggression within that group. Naiveté can make someone a victim. Therefore, he has to know how to use the language and attitude of hostility in order to defend himself against it. If you want to be an artist at self-defense, you learn karate, but only under the rarest circumstances do you use it. Andrews suggests that if a person is going to be bitchy, he must be awfully good at it.

There is a superficial attitude that most gays adopt, and there is also an isolation gays feel, not only from others, but from themselves. Because the gay often does not know himself, he reinforces his isolation. He looks at himself as a stranger, and he feels like a stranger within his own group.

GOTTLIEB: I think we're getting into something very profound here.

ANDREWS: The fast tricking . . .

GOTTLIEB: The fast repartee, the quick talking are ways of getting away from a very vital part of oneself.

ANDREWS: Yes. You substitute some of these things . . .

GOTTLIEB: For anger.

ANDREWS: Yes. Also for lust.

GOTTLIEB: You mean fast tricking is lustless sex? That sounds like a gay joke. Do you think gay jokes originate with gays, or from straights making fun of gays?

ANDREWS: The ordinary comedian before a straight audience sometimes puts gays down with "gay" jokes. But jokes are not humor. Humor is inventive, incisive, of the moment. I don't know how gay jokes originate, but I think they're from people with no sense of humor.

GOTTLIEB: I don't agree with you about all jokes because you think some of yours are funny, and so do I. Getting back to the gay and his friends and lovers—is there anything to be said for the idea that some guys are too selective?

ANDREWS: Like me.

GOTTLIEB: I think—I wish I could say this in a humorous or more sensitive way—you seem to be waiting for your knight in shining armor to come along.

ANDREWS: No comment.

Price has a lover, and I wondered how he feels about expanding his gay friendships.

GOTTLIEB: Do you think there's more friendship, camaraderie, and sharing of feelings in gay life?

PRICE: That's hard to say.

GOTTLIEB: Have you found it personally?

PRICE: I would say yes. And not from the fact that I'm with gays all the time, but because I find that there's more willingness to sit down and talk about these things, rather than hide them or shove them under the table. That's my experience and mine alone.

GOTTLIEB: Would you say gays are more sensitive to each other?

PRICE: I really think so.

GOTTLIEB: You're aware of the big machismo factor in gay life, but you've stripped that away and don't go chasing around to bars and orgies where everything is superficial.

PRICE: Let me interrupt you. Gay life on the whole, from what I have seen, is superficial—from the bar standpoint or places where people gather in huge groups—because everybody is a kind of commodity. There's interest in sex and maybe exploitation and a hell of a lot of insecurity. What irritates me most about gays is the phoniness and dishonesty of people who go into bars because they're interested in sex or in finding somebody to spend the night with. You can't find a long-term relationship in that kind of situation.

Bitch Queens, Destructiveness, Superficiality and Nellies

GOTTLIEB: So a long-term, sensitive, friendly, sexual relationship cannot be found ...

PRICE: In a bar.

GOTTLIEB: What you're saying is that there are some very superficial gays but also some with warmth and depth.

PRICE: Right. Whatever you call it, the gay community is so diverse it's almost impossible to type individuals as being this way or that.

Price is a sensitive individual who needs a great deal of attention and affection. Because of his inherent physical attributes, he has been able to obtain this without going to bars, orgies, or baths. He is a man who can successfully conduct himself as a gay without being involved in the bitchiness, superficialities, and other unpleasant qualities that we have been discussing. He does this by avoiding too much exposure on the public scene. He might be a good example to follow.

The bitch queen and the obviously gay man—the nellie— are often confused by gays and straights. The nellie may be bitchy, but it is his other characteristics that set him apart; and often there is a complete absence of the unpleasant, bitchy qualities of the bitch queen. A man does not have to be a limp-wristed sissy to be obviously gay. You may be absolutely certain that a man is gay, and you may be right, but you cannot always describe what makes him gay.

I have been equally at a loss for words when asked how I know a man is gay without knowing him personally. So have Andrews, Price, and Weber. The four of us gave it a lot of thought, and I have come to one conclusion: However the obvious gay behaves—be he butch, nellie, or somewhere between—somehow his personal behavior is exaggerated.

Maybe sincerely, maybe not; maybe knowingly, maybe not; he has a theatrical quality. Andrews's statement, "Gays are like everyone else, only more so," particularly applies to the obvious gay.

The less obvious gays have mixed feelings about their obvious brothers. Andrews thinks they can divert public attention from him, Weber thinks they are embarrassing, and Price thinks they are dull. I conclude that the obvious gay can be more of a pariah among gays than among straights. That may be because I feel no heterosexual threat from them and I am comfortable with them. I defended them against Andrews.

GOTTLIEB: I've found hostility and distrust toward obvious gays from other gays and from straights, but particularly from gays.

ANDREWS: When a gay signals his homosexuality he potentially threatens all of us because homosexuality is not popular. He may not be intentionally obvious but I think he is insensitively obvious.

GOTTLIEB: What do you mean?

ANDREWS: I said homosexuality isn't popular. I think it's stupid or insensitive to challenge the heterosexual community with it, especially if you want you and your kind to be accepted. To me it's a form of belligerence. Why be belligerent when you want other people to like you?

GOTTLIEB: But I've met some of your friends and they're obvious.

At this point Andrews blanched. I thought I had caught him in a contradiction, and he hates that!

Bitch Queens, Destructiveness, Superficiality and Nellies

ANDREWS: David, you're right. I've made exceptions for some close friends, but by God, they still embarrass me. As close as these obviously gay friends are, I don't mix them with my straight friends, or many other gays for that matter. Maybe this makes me a hypocrite, but look—did anything about me tell you that I was gay until I told you directly?

GOTTLIEB: No. It never occurred to me.

ANDREWS: I don't believe in being potentially belligerent by being obvious. That's my point.

Andrews is greatly concerned that he be masculine and that there be no mistaking him for an obvious, nellie gay. I told Andrews that in my experience obvious gays seldom seek psychotherapy. He commented that they are so preoccupied with being gay they do not need psychotherapy.

This reminds me of my analytic work with alcoholics. I always feel that while they are talking sincerely to me, their minds are on the next drink. That is why psychiatry seldom works with them. They come to me only for comfort, not for work. The obvious gay does not stick with me either. He can not keep his mind on the psychiatric work at hand, but only on his next trick. In spite of his unhappiness, he is uncompromisingly dedicated to the pursuit of being gay.

Weber, who is very much interested in maintaining his aggressivity and masculinity, says that most of his relationships have been with what he calls "passive" individuals. I concluded that he meant obvious gays but that he, Weber, was evasive about admitting it. He pointed out that often the one who plays the more feminine role by doing all the work around the house, actually is the one who controls the love affair.

93

WEBER: The same thing holds true in a heterosexual situation. A guy can have a wife who is a cunt. And then he's pussy-whipped. Well, she's just as ballsy as he is only she's different physically. But emotionally, I find it's the passive one who almost always has the power in the relationship.

I caught Weber in a contradiction when I asked him his feelings about obvious gays.

WEBER: I haven't known many. First of all I would hate to become friends with someone I would be embarrassed to run into and have to ignore, so I've avoided them. But my exposure to them is very limited. Often when I've allowed myself to know someone who is a nellie queen, I've found a really sweet person. The only reason I limit my exposure to them is because most of my friends and all of my clients are straight. It would hurt a nellie's feelings in a restaurant or someplace, if I chose to ignore him or give him the cold shoulder.

I pursued the point with Weber by asking him why he thinks some gays are so obvious. He replied that it's a deep-seated problem that he can not understand. He speculates that obvious gays are very frightened, shallow, and ill-informed. They signal their availability by being obvious. I have seen Weber in relationship to other gays, and I think without realizing or admitting it, he picks up the signal from the obvious gay and responds by dismissing their obvious-ness as passivity. Then he can become involved with them.

According to Weber, the obvious gay does not want the

responsibility of competing in the straight world. The nellie's attitude is negative, "I don't want the responsibility of competing. Therefore, I'll dress nellie; therefore, how could I ever get a decent job with a company and be promoted? They're not going to have a nellie chairman of the board or a nellie president." It is a cop-out.

GOTTLIEB: Very few people like this come to see a psychiatrist.

WEBER: I think they're really dumb. I mean, people who are not too bright and not too sophisticated dress this way because they don't know better. In fact, most of the nellies are from small towns and come to Hollywood and are quick to identify with Hollywood. They go to those cheap shops that sell a lot of that bad-taste gear. Pretty soon they look nellie and they just don't know. Another thing is that they are not socially mobile homosexuals either. Their dress and their attitude and their postures and gestures limit them so that they're not going to be accepted.

GOTTLIEB: I understand that they appeal to straying heterosexuals and also to very butch gays, and aren't threatening.

WEBER: They're no threat because they make themselves into substitute women.

Jim Price, in his quiet way, seemed to understand the plight of the nellie somewhat better than the other two men. He thinks they simply want attention.

PRICE: You know, it's particularly true about kids who get into gay life early. They've not had any straight experiences. They don't relate to girls. I think this is their way of achieving some kind of identity. Whether it's negative or positive identity, it separates them from the masses and makes people take notice.

GOTTLIEB: Even negative notice.

PRICE: Yes, but it would also attract another obvious person to them. I know this one kid who not only acts nellie but makes a point of referring to homosexuality among a mixed group of people. Nobody pays attention to him and he protests his homosexuality as if it were a virtue. He becomes overly aggressive about it. I don't know if he's compensating for a lack of security or what. I think so. I think he wants attention.

Jim Price pointed out another important factor. Such an individual stays around gays only, and is secure only in gay life or at gay parties. His existence is extremely superficial and somewhat unreal.

When I asked if such individuals are happy, Price suggested that they might be a little more happy at the present time because society has begun to accept this kind of behavior more freely, at least in metropolitan areas.

GOTTLIEB: Do they assume the role of a clown in our society or some kind of court jester?

PRICE: I'm not so sure. I think it's an identity thing. It's a way of saying, "I am what I am, and I'm not ashamed." But these individuals, I find them so affected, so superficial and into gay life per se—the parties, the drinking, the bars—there's no other context they can relate to. And then they develop a lisp and all of the various mannerisms.

Bitch Queens, Destructiveness, Superficiality and Nellies

GOTTLIEB: Is that developed, or does that just come to them naturally?

PRICE: I don't know. I think it's developed. I've seen other gay people go through whole personality changes when they become involved in gay life.

Price is repelled and uncomfortable with people who blatantly announce their homosexuality. He thinks it is a conscious affectation and a real turn-off.

GOTTLIEB: Are these people very satisfied with themselves?

PRICE: I think they've made a decision simply by virtue of the way they are, and they're going to live with it for better or worse. They leave no doors open. There's nothing to be analyzed because they won't allow it to happen. Whatever happens to them is their own doing. Besides, they would be very insecure by someone's suggesting that they might be happier if they change themselves.

In my opinion, if a person has character and substance he can be nellie and his substance will carry him. Andrews says that the hardest thing to say to a nellie friend is, "Come on, butch it up. I've got some straight friends coming over." A gay can like his nellie friend, but he does not want to be embarrassed by him.

All three of my collaborators are extremely uneasy about the obvious or nellie gay and insist that they are not like that. I feel that they are typical of most gays in denying any similarity to someone on a lower gay social ladder. Like all men, straight and gay, masculinity is always felt to be in jeopardy. It is an accurate but unpleasant observation of mine that all men have to use less masculine men as a projection of their own inadequacies. Less masculine men accuse the more masculine of focusing on their macho image to prove themselves. It's nice to have both kinds around.

Hard as it is for the nellies to recognize their own obviousness, many of them have made marvelous and talented contributions to society. Their substance and accomplishments should certainly be more important than any appearance of obvious homosexuality.

6

"I am gay"—
Leveling with Parents,
Doctors, Lovers, and Friends

All of us have secrets that we do not want to reveal to parents, friends, spouses, children, relatives, or business partners and associates. Unfortunately, too many people feel obligated to reveal their *sexual* activities in social situations. It is boring, in poor taste, and really ought to be kept to oneself—with one exception.

Heterosexuals seem to feel that the homosexual must confess everything. If he does not tell us we wonder, "Is he, or isn't he?" We expect him to be open so that we can accept him—or reject him as a contaminant. It is the only situation where we expect another to testify against himself. If he does not, we spread rumors about him. The worst offenders in spreading rumors are gays themselves.

It comes down to some fundamental questions: Should you announce your homosexuality to everyone? Should you be selective? Should you remain in the closet? Although the questions may seem superficial, they invade an American man's right to privacy.

Jim Price has difficulty talking about personal material with anybody. He is not particularly suspicious, but he is guarded, and he does not like to rock the boat too much. I realized I was touching on a sensitive subject by the nervousness of his replies.

GOTTLIEB: How do you handle your family? Your parents? How do you communicate with them about your sexuality? Do they know? Do you talk to them about it?

PRICE: No. I never discuss that with them at all. I think they do know but I couldn't swear one way or the other. I don't think it bothers them very much because they know me pretty well. They sense that I'm fairly happy with what I'm doing and fairly successful. They don't seem to see a problem in my life. They never interfere or try to interject their own feelings about anything.

GOTTLIEB: What about the family of your friend, the fellow you live with?

PRICE: Same way. His family stays out of the situation.

GOTTLIEB: Do you think it's best to keep this kind of separation from the family?

PRICE: I think so, unless you feel the person.... I don't want to hide anything about who I am, but I think I could hurt people who are thirty or forty years older than I am. I don't want to hurt them by saying anything about my sexuality. I don't think they want me to tell them even if they do know. They would rather that I not state anything. I think it would do more harm than good, unless you have the type of parents with whom you've always shared everything. I've seen kids with parents like that and it's a two-way street. If you open up with parents under other circumstances, a lot of harm can be done.

GOTTLIEB: By saying something?

PRICE: Yes. They may not understand. You have to take that chance. This is just my own point of view.

Price is evasive about his communication with his family. Even though he would prefer to tell them, it is obvious he cannot. There are very few gays who have leveled with their parents. Most of the time they keep their sexuality quiet and parry questions with characteristic evasion.

My wife, puzzled by a parent's not knowing a son's sexual orientation, suggested my asking Andrews about his communication with his family.

GOTTLIEB: Did your parents know?

ANDREWS: I had the idea that they knew but were uptight about it. What wasn't said, didn't exist. If I had divulged myself it would only have challenged them, and I think they would have denied it. More important, though, they didn't discuss their sex lives with me so why should I have discussed mine with them?

GOTTLIEB: What you're saying is that you're discreet.

ANDREWS: Yes, and if you open up you may be rejected.

GOTTLIEB: This is what I call lying with honesty. You should not tell the truth only to satisfy yourself because you may hurt the other person. A husband can gratify his own conscience but devastate his wife by confessing to an affair. By telling the truth he breaks through his wife's denial that this could happen to her. Denial is a sacred defense. Often when parents are confronted with a son's homosexuality, they'll deny it by saying, "Oh well, he'll grow out of it."

ANDREWS: I had a friend who told his indifferent parents he was gay and his father suggested that he take up golf instead.

I have always maintained that heterosexual marriage is really the only way, and anything that veers away from it is not a healthy approach to life. I discussed this with Andrews in a brief interchange.

ANDREWS: Straight or gay, you have to join the marriage club to belong.

GOTTLIEB: A straight reader should know that this makes a single man, gay or straight, very uncomfortable. I just realized that I've had this attitude toward some of my bachelor friends. It falls into a kind of evangelic quality regarding marriage, and I really don't like myself when I do that.

Andrews stays very much in the closet as far as his business is concerned. Why should he declare his sexuality to business associates or clients? They do not declare theirs to him. He thinks if he went public there would be an intrusion into *his* privacy and that of his straight business associates.

Weber added an interesting twist to this problem. When he was very ill recently, his family came to visit him in the hospital. He felt that he should have leveled with them before. Not leveling had kept them at a distance, and he wanted to stop lying to them. He admits that you run the risk of rejection, and that is why gays generally do not tell their families. Interestingly, he felt that his family has some inkling that he is gay, but even with his severe illness he could not tell them!

GOTTLIEB: Do you know any gays who have informed their families? What's the usual response?

WEBER: In most cases I guess it worked pretty good. I know cases where they even accept the lover, have dinner together, talk over marital problems, etcetera, but you have to judge your parents and how much they can handle.

GOTTLIEB: Have you heard of cases of out-and-out rejection?

WEBER: No, not really. Initial rejection and shock, then later acceptance.

GOTTLIEB: What about the idea that it's something that will pass and someday you'll get married?

WEBER: I don't think that happens too much. First, it takes a pretty strong person to tell his family, and a person that strong and convincing isn't going to give his parents a chance to think he's going to change. It's a risk, but one I think is worth taking with some parents. If they are genuinely loving and fairly sophisticated, I think it's advisable to consider it.

GOTTLIEB: Does it clear the air so that a person can enjoy life without its being a big secret?

WEBER: If you don't, you cut your parents out of a major portion of your life.

GOTTLIEB: You had the unique experience of having an illness when you wanted your parents around. There are other events in a person's life, like success, when we want to satisfy our parents and families and we want to share it with them.

WEBER: When I was sick I felt rather calmly that I would die. I wanted to tell my parents that I had loved them all along, and I couldn't let them know about it because I had to keep a good, safe distance. The reason I couldn't be close was that I couldn't tell them. At that time if they had asked me, I would have said so.

GOTTLIEB: But you didn't.

WEBER: No. I didn't.

Most people have a difficult time talking about their sexuality with their parents even when it is conventional. Weber says that if they are very loving and understanding, it is okay to do so. Unfortunately, I have seen very few cases clinically where people can level with their parents, either straight or gay.

Gays seldom tell parents they are gay. The usual process is suspicion or denial, or, as Andrews pointed out, a complete avoidance of the subject. If you do not see or think about it, it just is not there.

A common myth among gays is that they can improve their relationships with parents through psychotherapy. It usually does not work. What happens is that the patient understands his relationship with his parents and is better able to deal with them. The parents usually make very little, if any, change in relationship to the patient.

The concept of friendship and leveling between gays and straight friends is uniquely illustrated by Andrews and me. I have known Andrews for many years, but there have been periods of time when we have not been in close contact.

Much of the time he was making personal adjustments of which I was not aware.

GOTTLIEB: When you called me ten years ago, you told me something was wrong, yet you seemed to be standing off as if you needed me but didn't want to see me—why?

ANDREWS: I knew I couldn't visit you professionally because you are a close friend. I had so much to say and was so anxious for a solution that I was literally paralyzed in pursuing just your friendship. I had nothing but personal problems to talk about and really needed professional help.

Most of the people with whom I have had contact indicate that they do need the closeness of a family, of a relationship where they can unburden themselves. Because the gay is so alienated from his real family, his friends—and sometimes his gay friends only—become his adoptive family. This was Andrews's problem with me years ago; so I asked him about friendly relationships he has with gays, those that are more than just sexual relationships.

ANDREWS: There are plenty of friends to be found in gay life. Friends, real ones.

GOTTLIEB: If a person is gay it's often difficult to be frank and open among straights. He feels more comfortable with other gays.

ANDREWS: Of course. You share similar secrets and you're also close because you're outlaws together.

I think the gay cuts himself off by restricting himself to friendships—and to leveling—only with his fellow homosexuals. He must keep himself in contact with the larger part of society by establishing bridges with straight life. Part of it does involve a certain amount of leveling with people whom he can trust, and, unfortunately, there is a limited number of such people.

The person with whom any individual must level, almost by definition, is his doctor. I have had patients who withheld vital information necessary for their treatment because they were embarrassed or ashamed. They have paid me a considerable amount of money and have not taken advantage of my ability to treat them because they would not level. Many gay patients going to a psychiatrist or to a general physician hesitate about disclosing their sexual orientation.

Andrews felt very strong about this point. He agreed that a gay must provide an input of information to his doctor. It is necessary in order to give the doctor a base line so that he can understand and treat his patient. Andrews insists that a person knows more about himself than anybody else does; therefore he must tell the doctor all.

Weber was more direct in talking about his involvement with the physician.

WEBER: Once you level with your doctor about being homosexual, all of a sudden you feel that more or less he's on your team. You're using him as a physician is supposed to be used.

GOTTLIEB: So the important thing is to seek out a doctor who will respond to you.

WEBER: Who will respond to you not only as a physician, but who will accept you and take all things into consideration.

"I am gay"

GOTTLIEB: What about a gay doctor?

WEBER: I don't think it matters if he's gay or straight. If you're looking for a cardiologist you wouldn't go to a gay doctor who specializes in clap. I don't think that gives you the best kind of treatment. You should never make it a policy of trying to be exclusive by going to see a gay doctor.

GOTTLIEB: How about a gay psychiatrist?

WEBER: My personal preference would be against one. I'm afraid it might develop into some kind of intimacy. Would he really be leveling with me? I really might feel more comfortable with a straight psychiatrist.

The important point of Weber's communication is that at least one person should be confided in—the doctor. A gay should choose someone professional and objective who makes him comfortable and who does not pass judgment.

Next I asked Price whether he would be comfortable talking to a doctor about being gay. He said he is in very good health and does not go to one. He also said that he would prefer a straight to a gay doctor. The fact of the matter is that Price has not placed himself in a position where he has had to level with a doctor. However, if one is not as careful about such diseases as VD and hepatitis as Price, one might certainly have to be prepared to tell the doctor about homosexual contacts.

I discussed the problem of leveling with one's doctor with a urologist. He admitted to embarrassment in asking his patients about their sexual orientation because he felt it would be intrusive and patients might reject him. This feeling might be true of many good doctors who hope a patient will volunteer such information because it helps them treat patients properly.

The Gay Tapes

I talked with all three men about leveling with a lover. They agreed that there is a high incidence of tricking or cheating on one's lover. If one is tricking and the other is not, the one who is not may very well know what is going on but not want to acknowledge it. Often he is very happy just to get along. The point at issue is that there is no reason to confront, to level with the lover, unless you want to hurt him.

Gay or straight, if you make confessions to clear the air, you are changing the relationship and it is never the same again. You put a new demand on him or her, and a new dominant and subdominant relationship will exist because it is asking the lover to carry the responsibility too. Remember: Jealousy is a universal human quality.

The entire question of remaining in the closet is one that confronts every homosexual. I stated earlier that everybody has his secrets and he does not have to reveal himself if he does not want to. The need to come out of the closet and reveal oneself may be motivated by some kind of guilt or ethic that presupposes a kind of confession, particularly if one is doing something that is outlawed.

GOTTLIEB: Maybe this inquiry will make people question my heterosexuality.

ANDREWS: So what? Your sexuality is still nobody's business even if you do talk about it. Chances are nobody is interested anyway.

We concluded by agreeing that each person has a right to his own definition of privacy. Each individual sets his own limits, and it is impossible to generalize about how much or how little a person should say about himself. A further extension of this is that everyone has a right to his own inhibitions. He does not have to go along with the crowd or with momentary impulses.

It is appropriate to bring this up in relationship to the male gay because people who feel guilty and ashamed about themselves and their sexual practices also want to square themselves with the world. One of the ways of doing this is to be entirely too open. It is a confessional approach to life that may be very destructive to the individual.

I have noticed among a number of people, both gay and straight, an attitude of, "I've got a secret. Don't you wish you knew what it is?" This attitude leaves you open to criticism and gossip, and other people might avoid you because you are being infantile. Such people turn me off, and I have not found myself able, in turn, to level with them. They seem to be the first ones to breach a confidence. In other words, people who are extremely secretive about themselves often try to inveigle themselves into another's personal life.

One of the most intimate of all situations is the one between the psychiatrist and his patient. Even then the good psychoanalyst recognizes that if a patient tells him everything during the first visit, he is either very sick, has had a lot of previous psychotherapy, or is trying to scare him. There is a respectability to reticence, defensiveness, and privacy—a time to talk and a time to be silent.

When people are somewhat isolated from society, they build up communication systems among themselves. Some of it is good, but some of it is destructive. Andrews is superreceptive to other people's problems. He is constantly used and abused as a confidant and good friend. I find myself feeling this way toward him too, but there is a burdensome aspect to this character trait.

GOTTLIEB: Is there a tendency among gays to unload a great deal of neurotic material on each other?

ANDREWS: Yes.

GOTTLIEB: Would you or could you talk as openly to a straight friend?

ANDREWS: Yes, but most of my friends are gay—the people I see most. David, you too must have close friends who are your confidants. Like many gays I don't exclude straights from my life. I just don't see them that much. Some of my best friends are straights. Even you. But I no longer burden any of my friends with my problems as much as I used to because a person with problems becomes a bore.

GOTTLIEB: You're gay and you're receptive. Do other gays confide their problems in you?

ANDREWS: Some, yes, but once they do they've used me to the point where I'm not even interested sexually.

GOTTLIEB: True. If you become a confidant, you become antisexual. It's a turn-off. The more you become burdened with other people's neurotic behavior, the more they see you as they see the psychiatrist, in a nonsexual way. You cannot mix the two, although there is a tendency to do so. It's one thing to be someone's friend and intensify that friendship, and another thing to have that person use you to verbalize all his neurotic complaints.

ANDREWS: I've found out the hard way! You're in for a big disappointment if you expect to ball some of these people who come to you with their problems.

"I am gay"

Every man has his own philosophy of life. Every man is potentially able to give advice and recommendations, to listen very carefully and make interpretations. This is the reason we in psychiatry have so much competition. It is the only field of medicine where we run into direct competition with lay people. Usually the doctor's word is taken for granted by the person seeing the doctor, and his friends and family respect the medical opinion. Sometimes, though, when people come to see a psychiatrist they are challenged by their friends. Such statements as, "Why do you go to talk to that guy? Why don't you come and talk to me? I won't charge you anything," are made in an effort to undermine the psychiatric process.

7

Medical Problems and Gay Sex

The doctor is generally dissatisfied because he is always looking for a perfect patient just like his first one, the cadaver. The cadaver never talked back, he was neither gay nor straight, he had no sexual perversions, and he presented no problems whatsoever. He was completely passive and did not offer any resistance to the doctor's suggestions or prejudices.

I have found that many doctors, internists, surgeons, urologists, and even psychiatrists, become quite upset when a patient tells them about a deviation in his sexuality, particularly if it doesn't correspond with the doctor's own sexual orientation. Doctors tend to distrust gay patients because frequently the doctors don't understand the many, varied sexual relationships of homosexuals and may even fear the patient's "strangeness."

One of the purposes of this inquiry is to inform gays and

straights about male homosexuality, but there is certainly information that the general physician and specialist also need.

The best information comes from the patient himself. He must educate his doctor. He must give the doctor specific information about the type of sexual relations he has had, about his exposure to various people, and about the frequency of this exposure. Doctors can only operate on information that is given to them.

The most important thing I was taught in medical school is that the diagnosis is made almost totally from an accurately taken case history. The art of general medicine is diagnosis. A brilliant doctor can diagnose correctly; a mediocre one can treat. For a gay it is particularly important to give a total history to his doctor, particularly because many doctors are hesitant about asking questions regarding sexual orientation.

Male homosexuals minimize the health hazards confronting them. The gay is widely exposed to disease because he usually is in intimate contact with many people—often complete strangers. It has been my observation that most gays, no matter how careful they are, have had at least one disease from sexual contact.

Hepatitis is a dangerous, sometimes deadly disease, which at the least can make a person very sick over an extended period of time. Venereal diseases are presently occurring at a greater rate among gays, and, when not treated, cause much difficulty.

Another common occurrence among gays is a nonspecific urethritis, usually brought about by anal intercourse. Anyone practicing homosexuality, or, as a matter of fact, heterosexuality, should be well-versed in these types of diseases, their symptoms, and their treatment.

Andrews, who wishes he were a doctor and is competitive with me, is knowledgeable about the risks homosexuals face.

GOTTLIEB: Some of these diseases can really shorten a person's life.

ANDREWS: I don't think that means much to many young gays. As far as they're concerned, they don't age. Very few of them realize that something, a disease, might shorten their lives.

GOTTLIEB: That's correct. I think when someone is very much involved with himself and with the present, he's not concerned with tomorrow.

ANDREWS: It's not that you're going to die at forty-five instead of ninety-five, it's how long you can stay young. So if a doctor can make people see that disease ages a person more often than it kills, you'll convert a lot of guys into health nuts.

GOTTLIEB: Do you think gays are more careless than straights about their physical well-being?

ANDREWS: It's not that they're careless, rather it's a fear of discovering that they're imperfect and mortal.

GOTTLIEB: One of the other groups that is very guilty of this sort of thing is doctors. We tend to make the worst patients.

ANDREWS: Like all other narcissists—and I suppose we can talk about doctors as narcissists—they think that nothing bad can ever happen to them.

GOTTLIEB: I would have to agree that there is something rather narcissistic about being a doctor, but that's kind of a bitchy remark, Andy.

There is a considerable devil-may-care attitude among gays. They deal with things on an emergency or patch-up level. Many come to the doctor only after the fact, after they have developed an infection and not maintained themselves. Andrews described himself as a hypochondriac, but speculated about another form of hypochondriasis.

ANDREWS: Can a person be a hypochondriac and *not* take care of himself at the same time? Can he be hypochondriacal about falling hair, wrinkles, and his looks, but not about basic health?

GOTTLIEB: Yes. Such a person may be overly concerned with superficial minutiae, and totally avoid the common-sense, physical maintenance.

Andrews is also concerned with hygiene as related to sexual activities and strongly recommends avoiding contact with anybody who has just had anal contact. This is a very difficult problem in orgies and baths, and is one of the reasons for the high rate of infections like hepatitis.

Most gays do not learn these things except by bitter experience. Andy personally has had little in the way of venereal disease or nonspecific urethritis because he is careful.

From Weber, a man who has involved himself in a multitude of sexual situations, I accumulated more first-hand knowledge of the various diseases and their effect on the gay.

GOTTLIEB: What about getting various infections, such as hepatitis or nonspecific urethritis from sexual contact?

WEBER: You don't get hepatitis just by rimming. I did the research on it because I had hepatitis. The reason is that the aggressive male can get it without any oral or anal contact. You can get hepatitis just by being closely involved with other people.

GOTTLIEB: Yes.

WEBER: You've got to realize that all these risks are increased with compulsive homosexual behavior.

GOTTLIEB: Having had hepatitis yourself, is there anything you can advise?

WEBER: It's a compulsive habit of mine to immediately wash my penis and that, of course, immediately breaks the romantic aspect. But it's the first thing I must do. I try to do it within sixty seconds of any sexual contact. I've made sure that I've cleared my urinary tract of any contagious germs.

I would think twice also before going to a public bathhouse. This is one of the things that stops me from having anonymous sex. It was tough for me. It came for me as a result of having hepatitis. That's why I don't do it anymore. I learned the hard way to be extremely hygienic and give considerable thought to the people I'm going to be with.

I have to remember that I'm doing something that involves my health. It's no fun to be laid up for six months with hepatitis after being promiscuous.

GOTTLIEB: That's a hell of a disease.

WEBER: Yes. Nobody wants to touch you.

GOTTLIEB: In addition to that, you're quite sick, and sometimes it can be fatal.

WEBER: But any time you're in contact with somebody there is the possibility of picking up a disease, and it does not have to involve immediate genital-anal contact.

Jumping up and taking a shower may be inhibiting, but not as inhibiting as having hepatitis and being alone for six months. The problem is in not knowing who is carrying such diseases as hepatitis or gonorrhea. During part of the contagious period of hepatitis, a person is not jaundiced, weak or nauseated, nor does he have yellow eyes. He looks healthy. After infecting someone else he may show signs of the disease, and be followed by those with whom he's had contact during the previous several weeks. Hepatitis in particular has a long incubation period, fourteen to forty days. During that time the infected person is a carrier.

Weber insists that infections are more common in the dominant homosexual, the one who is the injector, the one who inserts his penis into the other man.

WEBER: The fuckor gets it more often than the fuckee, and that's why the bathhouse scene is bad. It's a good institution for recreational sex, but in some situations a person who is in the incubatory stages of hepatitis could infect fifty to God-knows-how-many people, literally. It's because of the anonymous nature of the sex.

GOTTLIEB: Yes.

WEBER: And you don't feel any compulsion to call the other person and say, "Hey, go get a gamma globulin shot. I think you infected me with hepatitis."

It would be absurd to try to discuss everything a homosexual needs to know about potential medical problems in this chapter, but if there is any question, the homosexual should see his physician immediately and *level* with him. Give him all the details. Even if it's embarrassing, no one can afford to gamble with his health.

There are heterosexual men who perform anal intercourse with women, get infections, and go to the doctor but do not tell him all the details. Many doctors do not ask, and some are even completely ignorant of variations in sexual practices. As sophisticated as I think I am, I hear something new every day. Patients and doctors must educate each other.

Price seemed distant and unconcerned about the problem when we discussed it.

GOTTLIEB: You're aware of the possibility of venereal disease, hepatitis, nonspecific urethritis, and all the other problems. Have you any thought about this in terms of gays?

PRICE: Not in relationship to myself. But I do think that gays are very promiscuous, at least the kind who have no relationship with one person and go out a lot. There is more promiscuity in homosexual life than in heterosexual life, maybe because we're so isolated by other members of society. You can be gay and enter into a sexual relationship without feeling exploited. You can't be as promiscuous in heterosexual life without being exploited.

GOTTLIEB: I see. A gay can just do it casually.

PRICE: Society really neither condones him nor condemns him.

GOTTLIEB: Is a gay expected to be promiscuous?

PRICE: I guess so. Yes, I think so.

GOTTLIEB: Do you think it's wise to be promiscuous?

PRICE: No, not from my standpoint. I think then you look upon sex as a mechanical act with no meaning.

GOTTLIEB: So you don't go in for meaningless sex—the trick, the orgy, the bath?

PRICE: Absolutely no. I just don't like it. It just doesn't appeal to me. I feel bad going into places like that. The person that you're going to spend the rest of your life with and going to be loyal to is somewhat affected also. On the other hand, I think it's bad to feel guilty just because you may get involved with someone else along the way.

Finally, in discussing some of the problems of the gay and his hygiene, Andrews pointed up a rather important concept. We do not have in our sex education anything about the physiology or anatomy of homosexuality. Very rarely do people know a great deal about their anatomy and particularly how they function sexually. How anatomy relates to homosexuality intrigues Andrews.

GOTTLIEB: Are gays ignorant of their sexual anatomy? It seems that with so much concentration on sex they should be well informed.

ANDREWS: I think straights get more sex than gays, but I think everyone is rather ignorant about how their bodies work.

GOTTLIEB: Don't you think gays should have some specialized knowledge?

ANDREWS: Yes, they should, but most haven't. Some people picture anal sex as just something dirty. Yet the male being penetrated can have heightened sensation because of the joke nature played on males—placing the erogenous prostate a penis-length up his rectum. Curiously, some gays don't know why they like being penetrated, but this is why.

GOTTLIEB: How much gay sex is anal? How much is oral?

ANDREWS: You've just limited gay sex to two methods. I can't answer the question and I don't think anyone can because what you do really depends on whom you're with and the moment. I think gays would not get as many contagious diseases as they do if they paid more attention to anatomy and physiology. Aware gays, as much as they want sex, often avoid promiscuous contact because of this. Still other men, in a combination of hope and consideration, clean themselves thoroughly inside and out before they go out on the town. No matter how you look at it, David, homosex is awkward, whether you're careless or careful.

GOTTLIEB: Yes. Unfortunately, the more you know about your body the more precautions you take and the less spontaneous you become. I assume that role playing is important, and a homosexual must be a very good actor to be hygienic as well.

ANDREWS: This paints a pretty grim picture of some homosex, but I'm handicapped by the carelessness of some of my fellows. If we gays made it a point to know our bodies and be extra careful about hygiene, we'd not have to fear for our health with every trick.

Here I agree with Andrews that even a little knowledge is worthwhile.

I have consulted with proctologists, urologists, internists, and dentists to compile the following information on diseases common to male homosexuals. All of these conditions require immediate medical care.

Syphilis:

Syphilis is usually first seen as a chancre (sore) on the penis. Chancres can also exist in the mouth and in the anus. The disease is usually spread via the penis when in contact with the mouth or anus.

Gonorrhea:

Infections are found in the anus and mouth and probably spread by oral and anal contact with the penis. The most common symptom is discharge from the penis.

Urethritis (Nonspecific):

This infection is caused by normal anal bacteria coming in contact with the penis during anal intercourse. Symptoms are itching and burning in the penis, and there may be a discharge similar to gonorrhea.

These three—syphilis, gonorrhea, and urethritis—are best prevented by decreased promiscuity and immediate cleansing of genitals after sexual contact with anyone.

Hepatitis:

The type of viral hepatitis most likely to affect the homosexual is the type existent in the digestive tract, and also, some doctors think, present in the semen. The virus comes through the digestive tract to the anus after being taken in through the mouth. There is an incubation period of about twenty-one days. After that time a person develops the symptoms of fatigue, jaundice, loss of appetite, and fever. This disease is never passed through the lungs or by breathing in the virus. Probably a mixture of oral and anal intercourse with strangers without adequate cleansing is the major causal sequence in gays.

It is contagious during the incubation period when there are no symptoms and the infected person becomes an unknowing carrier.

Condylomata Acuminata:

These are anal warts that are very painful and probably of viral origin. They are most probably spread by anal intercourse.

Proctitis, anal fistulas, or direct infections of the anus:

These are quite common, and all are due to injury to the anal and rectal tissues with subsequent tissue breakdown and invasion by bacteria ever-present in the lower digestive tract. Symptoms are anal pain, drainage, and excessive itching. The causes are frequent and indiscriminate anal intercourse.

8

Friendship, Love, and Coupling— Jealousy and Infidelity

Friendship, love, and work are, in the opinion of many, what life is all about. Can friendship and love coexist in a gay relationship? It perplexes me because a male gay depends upon other males for both. Most men, gay or straight, do not make friends of their love objects. They usually restrict their friendships to male companions. This makes the gay's situation a unique problem.

An ideal heterosexual relationship is one in which a man and a woman are friends *and* lovers. The combination of the two is hard to come by, but worth striving for in both gay and straight relationships.

Weber feels that the two cannot really be mixed. Price likes things uncomplicated and has successfully fused love and friendship, and Andrews refuses love without friendship.

Friendship and sexual involvement should ideally balance each other according to Andrews. A real friendship means you are not jealous of the other person but delight in sharing him with other people.

Weber so isolates love from friendship that he even isolates his lovers from his friends. He feels that one may have to sacrifice friendships temporarily for a lover and says, "You just cannot maintain both."

Weber says he feels strongly about friendship and hopes that possibly a love relationship or a sexual one can become a friendship, but he defiantly states that friendship seldom turns into a sexual relationship.

I think that because of his compulsive sexuality, Weber ignores the clues of friendship and treats people as sexual objects first. Once having done so, these people are devaluated. No matter how nice they are, he cannot elevate them to a level of friendship.

What Weber says is those people who want very quick immediate gratification of their sexual needs cannot wait around for a friendship to develop. Compulsive, ritualistic, overactive sexuality is the antithesis of a friendly relationship. Weber is unable to show his relaxed, playful qualities and broadcasts, instead, an air of tension and urgency. It is possible to relax sexually only in a safe, warm accepting environment, and only then can one have truly uninhibited, enjoyable sex. No relaxation, no orgasm. It is as simple as that. Sex is play; it is physiological and spontaneous.

Price summarized the necessity of mixing love and friendship by saying, "The *only* thing you have as a gay is friends." But the friends, if good, are worth pursuing because they have different interests and can enrich life. He feels that it is important to vary one's life and interests, to seek out people with different attitudes.

It is necessary to substitute this kind of friendship for family. Only in this context can Price experience any degree of sexuality, love, and deep relationships. In direct contrast to Weber, he has to be involved with people before there is any kind of sexual contact.

Why the discrepancy among the men I interviewed? Going into greater depth with Weber brought out some background material for his attitude. He said candidly that he did not even shake hands with his father. He has gone through life trying to get a male's attention and companionship. Sexuality, for him, is a way of sealing companionship, but he does not really want sex from a man. He wants the companionship. This might be true for many gays. At the time Weber was talking about this, he was depressed and said that to think about all this increased his depression.

As Weber began to accept himself as gay, he began also to accept women as potential sex objects. Then he began to feel that he was a more complete individual.

GOTTLIEB: Is it damaging to always think of yourself as a homosexual?

WEBER: It depends on where you want to go. For me, yes, because half of my friends aren't, and I can't talk to all of them about it. Sometimes that prevents my getting as close as I'd like to. They're not ready to accept it. It probably would turn them off to me. I'm afraid of that. It worries me from a business standpoint.

I have the strong feeling that Weber is promiscuous in

order to validate his own existence and to stay away from depression.

GOTTLIEB: The homosexual is alone and hates himself, but with other homosexuals he can say, "I'm not the only one." If he finally accepts himself, he can go on to explore other aspects of the world, even heterosexuality.

WEBER: From personal experience and observation you're right. Compulsive sexual behavior precedes or follows a period of self-hate. Whether it is the cause or the result, I don't know. Consequently, you need your physical self verified and you panic. If you are cut off for a moment you go into a deep depression. Which comes first, I don't know.

When Weber was in military service, he was not homosexually active. There he did not have to pay the price of sex for friendship and companionship. He feels that most of gay sexuality is a substitute for being lonely.

WEBER: It's an addiction.

GOTTLIEB: Addicts seek other addicts and they make up a culture.

WEBER: Sex can be a way of escaping yourself. I know people who literally can't go to sleep unless they have a trick every night. Very common. There are homosexuals who make a full-time business out of sex. They're often very attractive people. Many are on the verge of suicide or have made several attempts. You needn't probe too deep to find out that's bad business. It does lead to complete depression.

GOTTLIEB: Can a lover offer any kind of continuity?

WEBER: A lover can.

GOTTLIEB: Have you seen it work?

WEBER: From what other people say I thought yes, but from what I've seen, I think not. I think if the lover ends up being like a business partner then it's a different thing; but then I know gays who've been together for years and they've fought every goddam day.

Weber bases his feelings on the fact that he has an insatiable need to find somebody to be with him. He cannot stand to be alone; for him it equals loneliness. He cannot tolerate being separate.

Maybe he cannot tolerate himself. At the same time, his lovers do not satisfy him as friends, and he sees them only as lovers. He has really substituted sexuality for friendship. He will have sex with somebody to maintain a friendship, but never as an outgrowth of the friendship.

Andrews endorses nonpossessive affection. It is a feeling that is not really understood by most people, but for him it is very workable in gay relationships. He can engage in various activities with another gay—he can laugh and have fun, have that person for a buddy—and also enjoy having sex with him. For him, that is the ideal gay situation.

Price has actually been living out Andrews's ideal relationship.

PRICE: When people who live together get bored, they must realize that each person has to grow mentally by pursuing different interests. In other words, you can't do all things together without one person stifling the other, or without one person's jealously questioning what the other person is doing.

GOTTLIEB: And you have this understanding?

PRICE: To a certain extent. We don't discuss everything we do. Certain things are left unsaid.

GOTTLIEB: Do you think that's the best way, to leave certain things unsaid?

PRICE: Yes. For myself, yes.

For Price, this coupling works, but Andrews has not found a situation like it yet. He claims he is too picky.

One of the problems that comes up in any friendship or love relationship is extreme jealousy. Andrews feels that if you do not expect a relationship to last forever but just enjoy it for the present, jealousy can be minimized.

GOTTLIEB: In my clinical experience it's when jealousy and extreme possessiveness crop up that the relationship begins to break up.

ANDREWS: In my nonclinical but horrendous experience, that's precisely the case. It certainly has happened to me in its own distorted way. I was always striving to get what I wanted by my possessiveness. I was trying to capture somebody, hold him prisoner with a lot of cute techniques to make goddam sure no one else got to him.

GOTTLIEB: So that became a preoccupation.

ANDREWS: It became a terrible preoccupation until I realized I couldn't enforce my demands on the other person; I could enforce those demands I made on myself.

GOTTLIEB: Yes. What happens when you're policing the other person, watching him, jealous of him, is that you don't have any energy left to be *involved* with him. You become an empty, possessive, demanding bore.

ANDREWS: You're so preoccupied you lose your sense of self. In a way, you cease to exist.

Jealousy is usually destructive and often breaks up relationships, gay or straight. However, jealousy is a necessary emotion. All-giving, nonjealous people are taken advantage of, even by nice people. If someone does not stand up for himself, in one way or another someone else will take advantage of him. We must make demands on other people for a certain amount of consideration and faithfulness; otherwise we completely depreciate ourselves.

So many gay relationships break up because of jealousy that they seem to form a pattern—almost a way of life: Make a relationship, become jealous, break it up—in a repetitious cycle.

GOTTLIEB: I've seen certain things repeated over and over again in both heterosexual and homosexual situations. There's often a confrontation between lovers, an expression of hostility, and then an excited reunion. Supposedly, sex is great after such an argument.

ANDREWS: They may be seeking the Holy Grail of High Sex again. I guess it's a pattern.

GOTTLIEB: How important is this in homosexual relationships?

ANDREWS: To be possessed, rejected, to reunite, to resent; this is an intrinsic part of the act that seems so necessary to gay sex.

Once a certain pattern becomes established, one is obliged to continue that pattern, to imitate, to mimic, to act in a very predictable way. People who are pariahs in society tend to seek this simple mode of behavior. To be a good gay, one is almost seduced into being histrionic about sex and to overreact with jealousy. It is all an attempt to get attention and acceptance, but the game's just not worth the effort.

Gays go through tremendous anguish, meticulous preparations, and elaborate primping for an encounter they hope will be a relationship. Unfortunately, these relationships, these chance encounters in a bar or wherever, rarely materialize into a lasting relationship and at best are very fleeting events. A gay needs to ask himself whether the quick trick that he forgets almost immediately is worth the time he spends getting ready for it. Elaborate preparations do not create substance; one should find the substance first, then invest the time and preparation.

I presented my straight attitude about being married, having a home and children, and anticipating grandchildren. This insures some kind of immortality for me, a continuity from the past to the present and future.

Andrews said that the gay is under the same kind of pressure to build a family, to build relationships, and to mimic the middle-class marriage. For him, it is an absolute necessity to substitute friendship for the family, but he can *change* friends. If he is dissatisfied with a situation, he can more easily leave it. The straight situation has many more responsibilities.

In a subtle way this is the appeal of homosexuality. There are not the same permanent responsibilities. The gay is free to move around and change. He does not have to support a family, carry life insurance, put children through college, or support any of those burdens that heterosexuals have.

It would be tempting for a man to blame homosexuality for his problems. Price is one of the few truly handsome men I have met who accepts responsibility for being as he is and doing as he does. Bill Weber, equally handsome and sought after, uses his charisma to set up destructive situations that automatically make him a blameless victim. Andrews and I agreed that shifting responsibility by blaming outside factors makes one a nonparticipant in life, a bitter observer. "I can't make it because I'm gay," is not a good excuse for nonperformance.

He feels that the first question is that of personal responsibility. There is no room for absolute, simplistic answers, nor can we be successful in making friends or having love relationships or just living by blaming others. We must take the responsibility for our own activities and live life to its fullest whether we are straight or gay.

We have already alluded to the fact that gays count on their friends to give them support during neurotic or depressing periods. When you confess personal feelings to another individual, you can be sure that at the same time you will begin to resent him. Sometimes when patients first come to me they are very open about personal matters because I am a stranger and I am not going to judge them, but as they become more familiar with me, they read into the situation a fear that I *will* judge them because they've told me something about themselves.

When a friend imposes too many of his neurotic problems into a friendship it is bound to cause some difficulty. We all do use friends as confidants, but we have to guard against this human tendency to resent them because we've told them too much. The gay in particular has to choose friends who will not abuse the friendship by using the confidence as a weapon.

GOTTLIEB: Do you have gay friends in whom you can confide? Let's say the way a husband and wife in a successful marriage confide?

ANDREWS: Absolutely.

GOTTLIEB: Isn't every gay confidant also a potential competitor?

ANDREWS: Yes, and because of that you have to be very selective about your friends and very responsible yourself. Your friends are your only family, and if you're lucky and patient, you can have a good family.

GOTTLIEB: Is this adoptive family made up only of gays?

ANDREWS: Mostly gays.

GOTTLIEB: And no sexuality is involved.

ANDREWS: You would be awestruck by the absence of sexuality among most gays who are friends.

Psychiatrists are often concerned with the making of relationships. Recently, though, there has been a lot of literature on breaking a relationship, how to get a divorce, how to adapt to being divorced or widowed, etcetera.

Weber has had so many relationships that I feel he should be an authority on breaking them up.

GOTTLIEB: You were talking about the complications of getting rid of a lover or breaking up a relationship.

WEBER: Most of the gay books and all of the newspapers tell you how to make yourself attractive to land somebody, but you can get that anywhere. After all, it can take months and years to break up a relationship. That's a very boring, destructive kind of down-deep period for the gay person, I can tell you that. A straight person can go to an attorney and make a settlement, but a gay relationship is difficult as hell to get rid of.

GOTTLIEB: In straight life after the relationship is over, there are institutions and clubs where people can complain to new friends about their ex's. Organizations are set up for the divorced person or the widowed person in heterosexual life.

WEBER: Straight friends give sympathy in case of a straight divorce. Families and friends keep in contact with both parties and take the matter seriously as friends. When a gay person splits up, how seriously can they take one man's moving out on another one? You can't go in and tell your boss that you're going through a messy divorce and you're not going to be yourself for six months. Whom do you talk to? You can't talk to your parents.

GOTTLIEB: From a straight point of view, your remarks sound complicated and kind of overwhelming to me.

WEBER: I've had lots of intense, live-in situations, one after the other. Most of the time I spend trying to get rid of them after I've got them. I would like to be my own man. I would kind of like to be myself.

GOTTLIEB: Which do you think is better, kind of a quasi marriage or being by yourself?

WEBER: After six or seven years of trying to get rid of lovers, I think at the outset you should prepare each other for the inevitable fact that one of you may leave. It's not like a marriage with children and divorce papers. You can make the statement that you're together for the summer, you're both men, and you're not going to interlock forever.

You might find a partnership continuing, but I like to inject that at the beginning so that the end isn't so disgraceful, and boring and traumatic. Again, to me my friends are the main continuity in my life. I've never found a lover who offered continuity. I really don't expect to.

In Weber's statements there are obvious inconsistencies. He wants both friends and lovers. He has the capacity for attracting both, but like many gays he cannot amalgamate them. Beneath his charming exterior I felt tremendous conflict and sadness that touched me deeply.

It is necessary for a person to have both friends and lovers. It is most desirable to combine the qualities of love, friendship, and sexuality into one because it makes life less complicated. For the gay it is an extremely difficult proposition, and to be accomplished demands openness, understanding, and control of jealous feelings.

Weber, in a moment of wishful fantasy, confided his thoughts about an ideal relationship. He likes to start off by being up front, indicating that he doesn't know where the relationship might go. It might be only a passing thing, so why not spend some time together in an open-ended situation, something comparable to an open marriage?

WEBER: I find it difficult to communicate my attitude to other gay guys. It sounds like a great open marriage kind of thing. But then as time goes on, I find it's hard to maintain. People in one way or another try to make it more. Even though people enter into a relationship intelligently, it's hard to maintain. As long as you're completely honest and open, though, it avoids a lot of hurt feelings. You can try to make your decisions without being cruel.

GOTTLIEB: Are you jealous?

WEBER: No. Of course, that's a protection from jealousy. Under the old idea of an exclusive sexuality between two people, jealousy would be all-consuming.

GOTTLIEB: For you?

WEBER: For me? Sure. It was always on my mind. Now I never think about it. It's not a problem.

GOTTLIEB: If you think about jealousy too much, you can't do your work.

WEBER: Now I find that I couldn't spend the time to be jealous. And of course, again, the problem of jealousy among homosexuals is that it's so all-consuming, especially in younger guys, until they have enough experience to get over it. It's one of the biggest inhibitors they have. They go through the phase until they find out that it's a big waste of time. Many homosexuals have a compulsive nature, especially the narcissistic ones. We have a frequency of contact with people, so the possibilities for casual sex in one day are much more than in a heterosexual situation. And in the heterosexual situation there's a little more subtlety involved.

GOTTLIEB: There is.

WEBER: Homosexuals, because they're used to being undercover and beneath society, know how to do something quick. Hit and be gone!

GOTTLIEB: That's a good point. Most heterosexuals usually blunder a casual affair. I shouldn't say usually, but frequently they're caught or don't cover up.

The Gay Tapes

Weber said it is almost impossible to police a male lover, and you might just as well forget about it rather than allow your jealousy to consume you. I asked him if a relationship can be patched up after a jealous fight. He answered that it can, but you are just preparing for the next problem.

Weber's experience has been that jealous incidents reach a frequency where the situation gets out of hand, where one person tries to outdo the other until it gets so bad that you have to be suicidal to stay in it. Because there is this possibility for jealousy, Weber's advice is that gays should be prepared for the eventuality of the partner's having sexual contact with other people.

WEBER: As long as you know it's a possibility it doesn't hurt so much. The worst happens when someone insists he will never be unfaithful. This may go on for several years when suddenly you catch him. Well, that hurts a lot. You've really been disillusioned. You figure out, "For two years I've been badly cheated." You figure you've been a fool. You become vindictive and bitter, and you know you've been the victim of a hoax.

GOTTLIEB: In a heterosexual marriage it's entirely different. I think if people reassure each other it helps to maintain the relationship. Discussing it is good in a heterosexual situation.

WEBER: Yes, if you go into marriage. What about gay marriages?

GOTTLIEB: Let's talk about it now.

WEBER: There's a possibility that real gay marriages might be a viable thing. It might provide the security for some people that the conventional heterosexual thing does.

GOTTLIEB: Do you mean if it is recognized legally?

WEBER: Yes. A formally recognized thing. First of all, it makes you think twice before you tie the knot. People will be more sincere about it, and it might carry with it the advantage of lesser income tax and more mutually owned property.

GOTTLIEB: People might treat the intimate relationship a bit more seriously if there are legal advantages and if it's more difficult to disentangle yourself. You go to the trouble of formalizing something only when you think of it as being long term.

WEBER: Nobody is going to get married with the idea of its being for only a couple of years. You go into marriage thinking it's going to be forever. In this kind of situation you'd reassure the other person, but I don't know how wise this is in a gay situation.

GOTTLIEB: Why do you say that?

WEBER: If you need somebody and you know that you're not going to have children, the immortality of what you're doing sexually doesn't exist. But you're sexually attracted and you know very well you're both going to age and someday you're both going to be old. You won't have children or grandchildren. At that time a gay becomes attracted to a younger person. I mean, it's inevitable.

Gays sometimes handle this almost in a Greek way. You know, the coach-pupil. There always are some gay people who are very young and have no doubts about being homosexual, who will pair off with a man their father's age almost. There is some mutuality in that kind of relationship. It does complementary things. One has the experience, one has the youth, and one trades his youth for the other's experience. This has been idealized, but it has been victimized, too.

GOTTLIEB: But the unfortunate part is that the younger person will leave.

WEBER: Usually people say, "Well, you know, that dirty old man." But that's not necessarily the case. The younger person is going to gain the wisdom from the older man. He's going to grow up and out. The older man is going to find a replacement.

GOTTLIEB: He's got to prepare himself for finding a replacement.

WEBER: Yes.

GOTTLIEB: He can't keep this younger person enslaved.

WEBER: No more than he can keep anyone or that anyone can remain sixteen forever. You can't keep a child forever. He's going to grow up and out whether you want him to or not.

I pursued this question of fidelity and jealousy with Price. His responses to my questions seemed incisive and to the point.

GOTTLIEB: How long have you and your lover been together? Do you think of yourselves as a couple?

PRICE: About four years.

GOTTLIEB: Four years. So you are a couple. Do you think in that kind of situation it's best to have a relatively permissive atmosphere rather than a jealous one?

PRICE: It makes no difference what kind of relationship you have. If you can't allow the other person to pursue his own interests and grow by doing things different from the ordinary routine, the relationship becomes suffocating. I have to have an interest in sports, science, travel, and meeting other people. I think that's far better than when everything is centered around the home. I know people like that. Eventually it just won't work out. It just becomes too stifling.

GOTTLIEB: Why?

PRICE: You just lose creativity and become dull.

GOTTLIEB: Do people try to do that frequently?

PRICE: Yes. To lock in.

GOTTLIEB: And locking in carries with it the seeds of its own destruction, constant jealousy, and always wondering where the other person is. This is not the case with you and your friend?

PRICE: No. I think he'd be more jealous than I would. We just don't discuss it that much, and I think that the reason the relationship works well is that when I'm with him, I devote my attention to him. I think we're basically pretty respectful of each other. That's the thing that helps.

GOTTLIEB: Mutual respect for each other, mutual admiration?

PRICE: I think so. You know I've debated with myself for the last two or three years whether I really made the right decision living with this person—it's caused me a lot of frustration in the past—what other people would think and how they would react. Well, people I know in the neighborhood mostly are married and the same for the people I work with. I just keep wondering what they think. Do they think we're lovers or do they look on us negatively or "Why is he living there?" My position is that I just don't discuss those things. I don't bring them up.

141

GOTTLIEB: Do you keep your activities together?

PRICE: Actually we keep our activities pretty separate. We do that because people tend to pick up on little pieces of gossip, so our work and home lives are separated and it works out a lot better. I think a lot of people I know have nothing outside of the gay relationship. I think they're really very limited because they are able to go to bars or the opera, or do some of these things only with a group or with other people they feel secure with. I just can't limit myself to one group of people. I just couldn't do it. I'd be unhappy trying to do it, so I've made a lot of different interests. I've pursued friends and others in connection with my work.

Since Price has lived in a homosexual situation, he has disengaged himself completely from heterosexual experiences. He states that if he were not involved with one person on a homosexual basis, he would be more active heterosexually. I asked him if it would be deceptive to his lover if he had a heterosexual affair. He feels that it is not really deceptive and he does not feel guilty, but heterosexual relations upset him. It is the kind of emotional involvement that he does not want at the present time.

The question of fidelity, love, coupling, and marriage perplexes me in relation to the male gay. It would be very nice to have simplistic answers for these questions. I think it is quite evident that I was trying to twist the arms of my friends. I want them to say that the ideal model for heterosexuals and homosexuals is a relationship where people are sexually faithful to each other, where they get together in an equalitarian marriage, straight or gay, and where there are demands placed on each partner by the other.

These people do not agree, and now I have to defer to them. There are considerable differences between heterosexual and homosexual adjustments in coupling and faithfulness.

A double standard exists in gay and straight love relations. For the heterosexual, the concepts of open marriage, switching, and infidelity are not workable, not conducive to mental health or happiness.

Also many significant institutions are geared for the married person: schools, insurance companies, and social organizations. Weber thought maybe homosexual marriages could take advantage of these aspects, but he quickly gave up the idea. The prime emotional advantage of marriage is to allay loneliness by having a family and children and growing old together. The only advantage for the gay is the elusive conquest of loneliness. He has no children, religions reject him, and the IRS doesn't reward his gay marriage. He has all the guilt and unhappiness of the straight without the benefits. He has to answer to his partner for tricking or even his impulse to trick. It may be better to keep an open-ended concept for every homosexual relationship.

I have never heard of a homosexual, long-term coupling where there has not been some active outside homosexual activity with or without the lover's knowledge. To try to deny it would ultimately increase the upset. Either one or both of the partners will wind up right where he does not want to be—lonely, bitter, hurt, and angry—all of this without being able to discharge the anger through one of our best-supported institutions, the divorce court.

Those gays who try to mimic the institution of marriage do not have the societal supports to either maintain it or dissolve it. If the gay is lucky enough to find himself spontaneously in a long-term love relationship without all of the outside props, such a relationship borders on being sacred, particularly so if it satisfies his loneliness.

To force the issue and add demands is to diminish the possibility of real gay love. Certainly there will be exceptions to the statements I made above. I have not had contact with every homosexual, and there are people who will protest that they have had long-term, faithful relationships. But the rule is that temptations and possibilities for infidelity do exist. It is unreasonable to feel that complete fidelity can be assured.

Price came up with some interesting concepts about living in a homosexual coupling situation. He says that when two people feel guilty about their sexual orientation and are outcasts in society, they are going to express their jealousies and their promiscuity more directly. They will also be more sensitive about these qualities in their partners and more apt to find them. For these reasons gays have to tolerate more frustration and more infidelity.

Patience is necessary in all intimate relations. People just don't always do what we want them to, when we want them to do it. My own attitude toward life is simplistic. I feel that in a marriage the relationship should be equalitarian. This leads to the best of all possible worlds and to the highest degree of happiness. It certainly applies to the homosexual relationship. Nobody wants to be dominated and everybody wants to be equal. I was shocked, therefore, when Weber said that the best kind of coupling relationship is based on *in*equality.

GOTTLIEB: Don't you think there has to be mutual admiration, mutual respect? Would you agree that a relationship will fail if one person is destined to be prominent and the other person is nothing?

WEBER: No. Sometimes people can have their pleasure by taking someone else's strength and accepting that. They can find a perfect mate, accept the other person as a superior of sorts and share in that aura.

GOTTLIEB: What does the supposed superstud feel about the other person?

WEBER: He can be very respectful and loving toward the other person.

GOTTLIEB: Is there something about the other person he admires?

WEBER: I think just the fact that there's some love there, something. There can be respect in spite of the fact that the lover hasn't done a great deal with himself.

GOTTLIEB: He chooses a partner who gives him attention? Can it operate in just a one-way direction? Wouldn't he tire of this?

WEBER: It can exist that way. Gay people are not as much social climbers as straights are in choosing their mates. They don't mind that someone isn't particularly interesting. But given the attention, there's enough to sustain it. Eventually they'll break up but while it lasts, such relationships can be very satisfying.

GOTTLIEB: Most successful heterosexual marriages are based on mutual admiration. Each person accomplishes something. Each respects the other for his good qualities.

WEBER: It's not so with gays.

GOTTLIEB: You mean a long-term relationship may exist where there isn't mutual admiration, at least to the outsider?

WEBER: Look, Dave, the problem with the homosexual is

male competitiveness. Much mutual admiration can quickly turn into fierce competitiveness. You wouldn't compete with your wife in a lot of areas, but in an arrangement with a male, even a romantic one, that admiration could turn into fierce competition. So that's why you often see these strange couplings of homosexuals.

GOTTLIEB: That's new to me.

WEBER: It may be an aspect you haven't thought much about.

GOTTLIEB: No. I thought the opposite.

WEBER: What I do is always find somebody weaker than I. That's my protectiveness. I want to be the one who is totally financially sufficient, or more so. Also, in my career I want to be equally successful. I seldom have a relationship with anyone who is competitively close to me. I kind of do the opposite. I choose someone less successful, less strong in some way, so I feel that I'm the dominant one in the relationship.

Weber feels that this is the rule rather than the exception. The weaker person looks for the stronger. The stronger gay wants one weaker than he so that he feels more secure and dominant.

I asked, "If the two have an equalitarian relationship will there be more fights?" Weber felt that two equal males don't do as well as a male and female. His ideal marriage is to a lovely, subservient Polynesian woman. I replied that this idea was transposed from the homosexual to the heterosexual and in his actual heterosexual experiences, he has usually chosen an aggressive, dominant woman. Maybe that is why he remains gay.

Extreme competitiveness between people of the same sex

can lead to brutality. To avoid competition, Weber would not mind completely supporting another individual. He would expect warmth, tenderness, and insight from that person, and he would provide security, wisdom, guidance, and decisions in return.

GOTTLIEB: Then you'd play the total masculine role.

WEBER: Yes.

GOTTLIEB: You'd like that?

WEBER: Yes. I don't want anyone else pulling the role on me.

GOTTLIEB: Are you attracted to men who are more masculine than you?

WEBER: That's a tricky area to get into. Often the man who appears more masculine is a supercunt in disguise. I've learned a bitter lesson that way. I'm not attracted to effeminate men, but some have more female characteristics—positive ones—than others, and they can be very nice. I'm not as sensitive as I should be, and I've run into gay guys who have taught me a lot. They brought tenderness in and appreciation for things. I think that's valid and to be sought after.

In most cases that's what I tend towards finding—not an effeminate man, but one who tends to be less aggressive, less dominant than I am. I couldn't live with a dominant male, a competitive person. It couldn't happen.

GOTTLIEB: Is competitiveness a cause for concern in gay life?

WEBER: The first thing you have to ask yourself when everything else seems to be perfect is, "Is it competitive?" Sometimes you find out too late.

The Gay Tapes

As an analyst I often get caught up in trying to make patients' adjustments to life as good, if not better, than my own. I have to keep saying to myself that what might be good for me or what might be good for the heterosexual, is not necessarily good for the gay and his adjustment. We all often think that what *we* do, what *we* are, and what *we* feel is right, and what someone else does is quite wrong.

Weber's attitude did not ring true, and I was quite certain I would find the diametrically opposite point of view from Price. On the contrary, Price agreed with him.

GOTTLIEB: Do you think there should be some kind of mutual admiration, mutual respect? Don't you think that's necessary?

PRICE: Yes. Mutual respect and mutual understanding of each other's feelings. I don't think the relationship has to be fifty-fifty necessarily to be successful or on-going, but as long as that person who is less than fifty percent is aware that the other person really cares, it can succeed.

GOTTLIEB: What about mutual respect?

PRICE: Yes. Mutual respect has to be there. I think the reason the relationship breaks down is because people don't like themselves very much. But if you have respect for someone and he has respect for you, you kind of like yourself. Otherwise it's going to be hard to carry out a relationship with someone else. I don't think you can have someone bolster you all the time without your feeling, "Well, I've got to respect myself."

Price feels that a relationship is good only if it runs fairly deep. I think he avoided my point about mutual admiration, and substituted a concept of mutual respect which is probably much better. This makes allowances for unlikely kinds of relationships where people from diverse backgrounds get together and make it quite adequately. My Pollyannaish attitude about mutual admiration seems to have been put down at the hands of these two men.

Many gays who are extremely self-righteous get very little outside sex and are true to their lovers. They have established a pair bond with a lover and are extremely sentimental about their relationship. Andrews has some feelings about this kind of thing.

ANDREWS: The sentimentalist, who sets up his ads in *The Advocate* and asks for a true, deep relationship with a kindred spirit is kidding himself and advertising only his loneliness. To me, this guy is similar to the person who brags about how many tricks he's had, how much of a whore he is. The difference is our man is bragging about his righteousness.

GOTTLIEB: As a gay.

ANDREWS: As a gay, right. And when he's with a lover for any length of time, he's still not accepted by society. So he tries extra hard to make himself acceptable, perhaps to himself and he becomes righteous and blatantly ideal.

GOTTLIEB: So what you're saying is that either extreme, tricking or self-righteousness is an exaggeration.

ANDREWS: It's an ostentatious attempt to be more correct than anyone else.

In reviewing this chapter, I must raise some questions that supersede my previous conclusions and arguments.

Can any person grow and mature without a close, intimate, love relationship with another human being? Can you or I grow on fantasy? Must we have at some time in our adulthood, maybe even fleetingly, a true bond with another, stripped of fantasy? Or simply, is the definition of growth learning and relearning the art of intimacy and love?

Some gays never grow, but repeat the same behavior ad nauseam, embellishing a bit at times with some of the trappings of adulthood.

Such people are intruders into adulthood or play at being adult. Is the opportunity to slip out of a relationship so easy that one does not stick it out? If not worked out, the development of intimacy and love is made impossible. Does, then, personal growth stop?

When the sex gets bad or there is no sex, the affair is not necessarily over. One may be entering into the equivalent of a marriage where one deals with a *person*, not just with a body.

9

The Male Gay and Women

I have been interested in the gay male's relationship with women, and I have seen enough gay men being bitchy and hostile to straight women to wonder if this is not a tendency among male gays.

GOTTLIEB: How do you feel about women?
ANDREWS: They're people like you and me, but obviously I'd rather not spend time with them. That's about as productive as a gay guy's spending time with a straight businessman.
GOTTLIEB: Aren't some gay men particularly hostile toward women?

Andrews admitted that some are but said there are also many straight men who make a point of putting women

151

down. He had not answered directly so I pursued the questioning in another vein.

GOTTLIEB: I am referring to those people who advertise almost with a neon sign that they're gay.

ANDREWS: No, let me think. Sexists, gay or straight, are just people who look down their noses at anyone. Because a gay looking down his nose is so obviously a gay looking down his nose, we can jump to a conclusion that only gays are antiwomen.

I think there is generally a great deal of hostility that men, heterosexual or homosexual, feel toward women. One's primary childhood figure is the mother, and it is toward her, the female authority, that most feeling develops—much of it hostile. Women feel this way toward their mothers, straight men feel the same, and so do gays.

In adults, these childhood hostilities linger on. Let me give you an example. A group of men go into a restaurant, the waitress comes up to the table, and they make remarks with *double entendre*—sometimes blatantly sexual remarks. They treat the girl with scorn and ridicule. We sometimes do not see this as male hostility toward women, but it is. I do not know if this is as frequent with gay people in the same situation. I would guess not, because since they are gay they do not have to prove themselves by bullying women.

ANDREWS: I say this for myself, David, and I think I say it for other gays. A lot of them enjoy women in a casual situation and probably get along better with them than straight guys. Maybe the reason is we are not on the make, have nothing to prove and have no axes to grind.

Fortunately, most heterosexuals get along with the opposite sex and so, for that matter, do most homosexuals. The ones who do not, straight or gay, have one thing in common—they cannot forget their grievances, real or imagined, against Mama. This is a neurotic attitude very common among straights and gays, but straights tend to deny it and say it is a gay trait. "He has a thing for his mother. That's why he's gay." It is another attempt to blame the woman.

GOTTLIEB: Do you think some women find homosexual men hostile just because they're uncomfortable with them?

ANDREWS: That's a professional's point and I can't disagree. Also, straight women often feel a sense of competition with gay men for other men.

GOTTLIEB: I've had female patients say to me they're hostile toward gay men because there are not enough men to go around in the first place.

Several of my discussions with the men in this work led to the feeling that if you can accept yourself as straight or gay, then your orientation toward women improves. Andrews indicated that when he accepted his homosexuality he could deal more effectively with women. He became at ease with them and with other people too.

GOTTLIEB: If a person does not fight his homosexuality or deny it, he can make better heterosexual relationships.

ANDREWS: Are you talking about sexual relationships?

GOTTLIEB: No, just a better communication with women.

ANDREWS: For me that's been true. I can be friends with women because I am not interested in being their lover. David, I said before that I believe lovers should be friends in gay life. Does this admission make me a hypocrite?

GOTTLIEB: No. It makes you gay—and just a little more human.

I asked Andy if he felt that gays make good heterosexual lovers. He replied that the ones who do, do so because they are detached enough to focus on the techniques that satisfy women. In terms of techniques with women many gays are better than straights. What they lack is feeling. They are as good as whores.

Earlier Andrews mentioned a lengthy affair he recently had with an attractive, promiscuous woman. As he described it I pictured her as a pleasurable emasculator dehorning each man as he came. When this woman discovered Andrews was gay, she not only immediately dropped him, she also denied a great part of their sexual involvement including her constant praise of him as a lover.

I think her hysteria was caused not by her castrating another man, but by her being pleased and bamboozled by what she would see as an already castrated man—a gay. In my opinion, she, an otherwise reasonable straight, had neurotically felt she made a fool of herself. Andrews thought, however, that she became upset after all that time because he had made her feel like a lesbian.

Weber was quite concerned with his own masculinity. He said that a gay, in order to prove his masculinity, might even try to impregnate a girl. He admits to having tried it himself but at the present has more respect for women than he used to, and would not use them to prove himself.

GOTTLIEB: Do you think gay men make better heterosexual lovers?

WEBER: If they can do it they may be pretty good. The girls I've slept with could never understand that I was gay. One girl I know admits that she prefers bisexual men. She says that they're more sensitive than the straight guys. I feel she has a thing about turning on gays, but that's an exception with gay guys. Most of them are exclusively gay. I guess only about ten percent are bisexual. Most are kind of revolted by a woman's vagina. I suspect that maybe ten percent could establish a fairly good relationship with a woman.

GOTTLIEB: What is your feeling about women in general?

WEBER: They're fascinating. You can't help having dealings with them at some time or another. I think gay people try to cut them off completely. Most gay guys want nothing to do with women at all. They can only be threatened, or they'll be cunts or this or that. They have a million reasons not to have dealings with women. I think that a gay person should think of the possibility that he might be a closet straight, you know. At some point in his life, maybe he will find himself—he can't conceive of it—but all of a sudden he might be attracted to a woman. In the midst of a heterosexual—even in the midst of a homosexual—relation, why should a person limit himself?

Weber had some very strong feelings about Gay Lib and said that he would not want to identify himself and walk down Hollywood Boulevard holding a jar of Vaseline. He wants to leave all options open, he does have positive feelings toward women, and he would like to continue to have some heterosexual contacts rather than cut himself off completely by identifying with any gay movement.

Since I've presented the point that homosexuals should be involved with women and that a certain number of them possibly can have heterosexual relations, another question presents itself. Is it really fair to become seriously involved with women if you are gay? Is this a right thing to do? In order to answer this question I talked to Price at some length.

GOTTLIEB: Do you go out with women?

PRICE: I do, but I haven't had any sexual relations in quite awhile. It's something I miss to a large degree, even though I'm more comfortable around men.

GOTTLIEB: Why don't you?

PRICE: Right now I feel it's tough for me to develop a relationship with women while I have something going in the other direction. It would be hard to reconcile this in my own mind.

GOTTLIEB: Would you feel dishonest?

PRICE: It's not a question of divided loyalty. It's too much to handle, too confusing. I tend to block it. At this point in my life I feel that I should stay with my present decision.

GOTTLIEB: Do you think—not just for yourself but also for others—do you think there's anything wrong with being married and homosexual?

PRICE: I know it's common.

GOTTLIEB: I don't think we like to admit how common it is.

PRICE: Exactly. It seems quite common among the upper echelons of Los Angeles society. If a person can find it, fine. But it seems to me that kind of person can't find any relationship that works.

GOTTLIEB: It falls then within your concept of promiscuity?

PRICE: I think it's unfair to decide to be married and to have no commitment, but to have the license to do whatever you want. Either you decide to be married and be straight, or you decide not to be straight and have relationships with more than one person, maybe male and female.

GOTTLIEB: But you're not a person who can have an affair with a girl without being sincere? Or with a man, for that matter?

PRICE: Yes. I'd have no way of reconciling that in my mind.

GOTTLIEB: Let's extend this a bit. What if a man is homosexual or has homosexual impulses and decides to get married. Is it wrong to get married? Let's say he can function with women but he's not entirely sold on them. Can he be happy staying away from homosexuality?

PRICE: Maybe he feels marriage is more secure to him than the homosexual relationship. He should think of his wife and what she has to put up with. I think this kind of thing exists, but I don't have any close friends who have been able to handle it successfully. I just think that generally it doesn't work. A guy can maybe get frustrated and start going out on the side. It becomes kind of an obsession. You cannot have a good heterosexual and home relationship unless it is first and foremost.

The Gay Tapes

Bill Weber recommended earlier that homosexuals keep heterosexual contacts open, if for no other reason than to broaden their perspectives. He had some other feelings as to whether you should level about your homosexuality if you are in a relationship with a girl.

GOTTLIEB: What do you think about giving a girl an explanation about your homosexuality?

WEBER: She should be aware. Can you imagine a girl who's gone out with a guy—let's say she's gone to bed with him—it's hard for her to imagine he's homosexual. I don't think she thinks about that. And all of a sudden he drops her. She can't understand why until after. But let's say she knew at the onset that he was gay and they ended up together in bed having a ball. It probably would be more likely to happen this way than if I deceived her by presenting myself as straight. I'm afraid of that, because I'm afraid later she would say, "You deceived me," or something like that.

GOTTLIEB: Yes.

WEBER: So as painful as it is to be honest at first, if you're getting involved in any kind of relationship beyond recreational sex, I think you should level.

Fantasies during sexual activity are private, personal business. If fantasies do not correspond to what one is doing and cause guilt or anxiety, one may not function well. An extreme example for a gay is fantasizing he is with a man when he is actually with a woman. At that point he might consider psychiatric help.

Certainly it is all right to engage in recreational sex without revealing everything. One need not reveal everything from the past in a permanent, long-term relationship

158

with another adult, male or female, either, but one must be up-front and sincere about current feelings. Marriages of convenience must have the agreement of both parties to work. If they do not, the results are tragic.

It is a person's own privilege to sit on a fence about his sexuality forever, but it is not fair to ask someone to keep him company there while he tries to decide which way to go. If he does, he is taking unfair advantage of the other person's neurotic problems.

The male homosexual's relationships to straight women stimulated Andrews to comment on gay women.

ANDREWS: Gay women are still more socially acceptable than gay men. Straights hate sissies and gay men are still sissies to them, but straights like toughness and they think gay women are tough so they accept them more easily.

GOTTLIEB: Well . . .

ANDREWS: There's no such thing as a sissy girl. The antithesis of that, the tomboy, delights straights. A child lesbian is really the apple of daddy's eye. Tomboys, child and adult, get away with more than males. Even in today's swingers' groups, there is an acceptance of homosexuality among women, but a rejection of it among men.

GOTTLIEB: Would you be more explicit? I don't quite understand.

ANDREWS: The swinging groups, the heterosexual swinging groups. They orgy a lot and in this context female homosexuality is a turn-on while male homosexuality is a turn-off. Gays aren't the only men who revere the macho image.

Why is women's homosexuality more acceptable to straight men? Probably the quickest explanation for it is that men like to think of women in wild, sexy, orgiastic poses. It is a kind of sexual turn-on for the heterosexual, and may feed into his masturbatory fantasies. Under certain circumstances men like to see their women uninhibited. They like to be passive to such women, but do not like to recognize it as passivity because passivity is equated with femininity and femininity with homosexuality, and that is terrifying. In heterosexual orgies female homosexuality is allowed, male homosexuality is not, probably for the reason just stated. Heterosexual guys panic at the thought of any male homosexuality, particularly if it gets close to them in an orgy.

Another group of women who appear on the gay scene are the "fag hags."

ANDREWS: Fag hags, fruit flies, women who avoid heterosexual relationships and find safety in associating with gays. They'll have little sexual nourishment, but they stuff themselves on bright social tidbits of the gay scene. It's a one-of-a-kind diet. Rather fruity.

GOTTLIEB: Are they more a part of today's gay life than yesterday's?

ANDREWS: Per se, no. More visible, possibly. Look, David, gay is fashionable today. Gay baths, gay discos generate new show business names and have themselves become box office for heterosexuals. It's a phase in fashion we're all going through. It's called gay chic. It's developing into bisexual chic and one of these days heterosexual chic and bisexual chic will have their hours. But today many people are fruit flies. To one degree or another we decorate one another's lives.

GOTTLIEB: Would you recommend making such a person a confidante?

The Male Gay and Women

ANDREWS: I can't think of a decorative person being a warm, sensitive, human being.

GOTTLIEB: Do you think that they would really hurt you in some way?

ANDREWS: I think that whether they would hurt you purposely or not is not the point. I simply don't think that they would be capable of any depth or help.

A fag hag is like a white person who hangs around blacks, trying to talk the black idiom or with the black inflection, or trying to be a white-black. She thinks it is cute.

An obvious question is the male gay's relationship to the lesbian. According to Andrews these friendships are tenuous but they have patterns. The more masculine women seek the more feminine men while feminine lesbians get along well with masculine gay men. Tenuous and rare though these friendships generally are, sometimes they become deep.

Women homosexuals pair bond or marry more frequently, and they tend to live together for a longer period of time than male homosexuals. There are very few male couples who stay together for more than a couple of years. There are other discrepancies between lesbians and male homosexuals.

GOTTLIEB: I guess women are never arrested in bathrooms.

ANDREWS: No. It's awkward for a woman to stand at a urinal.

GOTTLIEB: Be nice, Andy. What's the real difference?

ANDREWS: I think gay women get to the point of homosexuality better than gay men—hearth and home. They tend to build their relationships around a home almost directly making up for the lack of affection in their childhood. Their sexual activity seems to take second place to their primary need for love and stability. They may abhor men, but they want the stability a man should provide. They simply get it with another woman. That's the difference between us—priority.

GOTTLIEB: In my experience fewer women homosexuals come to see the psychiatrist, but many male homosexuals come in for that very reason—loneliness and trying to find a stable environment.

Andrews feels that the only real commonality between the female gay and the male gay is the fact that they are both gay. They choose people of their own sex and beyond that, one is utterly female in orientation, and the other is utterly male. There may even be some hostility between gay men and women. The groups are without any deep commonalities and seldom mix.

When I asked Weber about his feeling toward lesbians he confessed that he really does not understand the problems of women. The relationships are so complicated that he has no feeling about lesbians, and he has had very little association with them.

Price also wanted to stay away from the question because he really does not understand it.

GOTTLIEB: Do you want any contact with lesbians?
PRICE: No, I'm not interested.
GOTTLIEB: You prefer a heterosexual woman?
PRICE: Definitely.
GOTTLIEB: How is it that you don't care for gay women socially?

The Male Gay and Women

PRICE: There's something about a really masculine woman—and most of them are—certain characteristics that just aren't attractive. They look down upon men and they tend to isolate themselves in the other direction by being very butch, tough, and coarse. I don't find them easy to relate to. They're not very attractive people.

GOTTLIEB: How do you feel about Gay Lib?

PRICE: I think it's a way of drawing attention to one's personal business. Things should be left to your own discretion. If you wave a banner for this cause and that it may be legally productive, but it's more out of publicity than out of sincerity.

10

Homosociality

A gay chooses a member of his own sex as a sexual object, but another real concern is to choose somebody as a *social* object. The *social* aspects of the relationship are much more important than the sexual ones. Sexuality comes in as a physiological and psychological necessity.

At no time could I or my three subjects tightly define homosexuality. It defied description as it covered such a wide area of life, sexually and beyond. In a moment of clarity Andrews said, "We're not homosexuals; we're homosocials." I felt that this was a remarkably insightful definition especially in terms of the highly elusive one-to-one relationship—that ideal, deep brotherhood that transcends sexuality to nonerotic love.

Weber, the man who has had great conflicts in this area, says that being homosexual does not necessarily mean everyone is a potential sex partner. Warmth and comfort with another person is satisfying enough.

Weber seemed tired and upset during this interchange.

GOTTLIEB: You seem kind of out of it today.

WEBER: Just overtired, and I started looking at homosexuality. It's a high price to pay for friendship, and that's really basically all I'm doing with it.

GOTTLIEB: I don't know if this goes across the board, but I think so. Men—gay and straight—really hunger for masculine companionship. There's a homosexual component in every man. I don't think a man's life can be complete without male friends, not that he has to see them all the time. Sometimes when I counsel women before they're married I ask about the fiancée's male friends. I find the reply a good indicator of whether the marriage will work out. I think a man does need male companionship. Often a couple returns to my office for counseling, or they consider getting a divorce, and I am not surprised because neither one had friends of the same sex. Women must have friends too. I'm very suspect of women who don't like other women and of men who don't like other men.

When Weber was a marine, he claims he went without homosexual contact for four years.

WEBER: I really found out I was gay in college in my twenties. I canceled out of school and decided to leave California to seek my fortune in Las Vegas. I ran out of gas and joined the Marine Corps. I found in the Marine Corps I had no homosexual drive whatsoever. So I can only say that while I was in the Corps there really wasn't a lot of sex for me. I didn't exactly come on though. I found that just the availability of male companionship satisfied me. I feel it's the same in society today. Why don't we have cavalry as we did in the old days? Or men jumping a freighter and going to sea? Not really for sexual purposes, but for those men who found it impossible to make it through a traditional, heterosexual, family-oriented life.

GOTTLIEB: Men find each other's companionship very good, and that is what Women's Lib doesn't understand. As a doctor I may be involved in a professional situation with a woman doctor, but I wouldn't choose to play cards with her, go to a football game, or sit around and shoot the bull. I'd choose a man. It's a rare situation where a man finds his wife a true companion and friend. This is unfortunately a sad testimony to marriage. Mine is rare and lucky because my relationship with my wife is a very friendly one. At most heterosexual gatherings men and women split up. Men talk about business on one side of the room and women talk about children and clothes on the other. There are some men who become agitated and nervous if the groups are not split up. They resent conversation involving the total group and can't function that way. Sometimes there is a sharing of information that I think is very good. There should be more friendship between the sexes!

WEBER: Well, that to me replaces the need for physical contact with men. And now that I'm on to that in myself, now what I intend to do is have a lot of comrades, straight and otherwise. I don't think I will need so much physical contact.

GOTTLIEB: I understand.

WEBER: It took me a long time to find out, and I arrived

at it by going back over my Marine Corps experiences and asking why I didn't have more sexual drive. I was young and in the best of health, and I realized it was quite enough for me. I got encounters, maybe companionship, from the other marines. Now I'm operating on a different principle. I do have more companions and I don't have all those compulsions. Things have changed quite a bit.

Of the three men with whom I worked, Price had the most to say about a "homosocial" life-style. After he had been involved and hurt in a very destructive heterosexual relationship, he began looking for an alternative.

PRICE: I was looking for kind of an out for all that game playing and ego competition, and I just thought I needed somebody to accept me for who I was—someone who really wanted to care for me, with whom I could really feel comfortable. You know, the person I'm living with, we're totally different people. He's much more involved in some things than I am. I guess you could say that he's much more gay appearing than I, but at the same time we've been very successful. We have different interests in different areas. I pursue interests outside of his sphere, and he is the same way, so we really don't clash in that area. He's very kind and giving and very accepting. I'm that way too. It's been good from that standpoint. It's really helped our security in the gay situation. It's hard to describe. I feel much more security perhaps for the wrong reason.

Five or six years ago Price went to gay bars frequently, but he did not get any pleasure out of it. He describes meeting some people, but the anonymous, fast sexual relationship was not satisfying.

PRICE: One of the secrets of my happiness is that sex is not an overriding consideration. It is an important thing in my life, but at least it's under control. It doesn't dominate my very existence.

Whenever Price has been involved in any kind of sexual activity, he says friendship and camaraderie were far more important to him than sex. He is a man who requires a considerable amount of understanding and sensitivity, not one who likes to talk about his own emotional problems. Consequently, when he does find himself in a homosocial situation, he is very comfortable and feels fulfilled.

PRICE: I don't try to analyze things in great depth, but I try to work them out myself. If I can't, I try to bring the problem out, but one of the last things I would talk about is my personal life. It's kind of a defense mechanism on my part. I think I talk about it more freely with gay people than with straights, probably because there's kind of a ready listener there. There are more communications and I think I feel more at ease in that kind of situation. I have a hard time talking about gay subjects with straights. I wonder what they're thinking or what impressions they have of me. I'm afraid of losing a friendship.

GOTTLIEB: It's difficult for straight people to understand the emotional problems of the gay.

PRICE: That's what I was also going to say.

GOTTLIEB: Actually there's nothing so great to understand. I think it's really very much the same for straights. We don't like to recognize that and it bothers us.

It was enlightening for me as a psychiatrist to draw strong parallels between gays and straights. I think to a straight, a gay's relationship to a lover sounds like a relationship to a woman. But we tend to resist recognizing this, both ways, and it may be one of the fundamental reasons that gays and straights misunderstand each other. People of different interests hate to see their similarities, and so we institutionalize uniqueness. We like to be different. If you really want to hurt my feelings, tell me you know someone who looks and acts like me. An exception, in my case, might be if you said I looked, acted, and was as brilliant as Sigmund Freud.

I asked Price a direct question to test the concept of homosociality.

GOTTLIEB: Do you enjoy homosexuality more than heterosexuality?

PRICE: Sexually, no. I'd say on an overall basis as far as knowing the people that I now know, homosexuality has been more rewarding for me. I've met people with more substance in gay life, I think simply because a lot of people I've always known have been straight. I've got two really good friends, who of all the people I know, are still married. They have really good adjustments to life—kids, and the rest. The rest were all looking in the wrong direction. They just weren't happy with what they were doing, and I think the relationships just wouldn't sustain themselves. I kind of drifted away from those people. It's hard to say what happened.

GOTTLIEB: So you would say you found firmer friendship in gay life?

PRICE: More sensitivity, and more of a willingness to know who you are as a person. I just found myself able to be much more open about the things I felt—much more open than I could be with people I had as close friends two or three years ago. I'm really afraid to open myself to even my best straight friends, because I'm not yet to the place where I feel confident to discuss these things with them.

GOTTLIEB: So now you prefer for your own emotional comfort, homosexual relationships?

PRICE: That's right.

GOTTLIEB: And it's primarily not the sexual aspects, but . . .

PRICE: I enjoy that more now than I used to, but the thing that I really couldn't handle about the other was the emotional aspect. I guess I became overly emotionally involved and less able to put things into perspective with women.

GOTTLIEB: So in other words, life has allowed you to keep a distance?

PRICE: Yes, it has. I guess it's a protection kind of thing. I've never really told people other than gay people, but I never told other people what I do. They raise questions periodically. I never volunteer anything unless it's necessary for them to know, but I am much more comfortable.

Andrews seemed to express himself best and most explicitly in terms of being homosocial.

GOTTLIEB: What is the feeling you have that makes you homosexual rather than heterosexual?

ANDREWS: You're not talking about the mechanics?

GOTTLIEB: No, attitude. Whom would you rather be with, men or women?

ANDREWS: Men.

GOTTLIEB: Tell me, Andy, do you perceive a man as a woman does?

ANDREWS: Perhaps, particularly as a woman finds the male body attractive, so do I find it attractive. You might say that makes me a woman. It doesn't. It's male, and it's a body. That's the physical side of it. The firmness and the male physique are as attractive to me as they are to the heterosexual woman. That's not the be-all and end-all of it. The other is the identity process. We think of it, this identification, not only in terms of sex itself, but in terms of being brothers, being similar. Instead of complementing the physical and emotional differences as one does in heterosexual mingling, in our way we match and there's a homosexual mingling. I'll state it as a wish: It's a wish to be like the person with whom you mate, with whom you're having sex, or with whom you're mingling. It goes beyond sex but includes it. I think "identity" is the word you would use, David. To identify with. You can rationalize this and explain it. Hell, I understand the mechanical nature of my male sexual feelings, the orgasm. I'll never understand the sexual feelings of a woman because that's something I, as a male, can't experience. I think homosexuality is just more agreeable to me. I think I delight in the differences between people and the similarities between men. I delight in the imagined if not the actual qualities of the other man. He can be me and I can be him if only for a moment. We are both men and there is nothing womanish about it. I never want a substitute female.

Homosociality

GOTTLIEB: Another gay is not a substitute woman?

ANDREWS: Of course not. That's the point, but if you ever want a woman, you find a woman.

GOTTLIEB: Does this mean that you'd like to be with men rather than with women socially too?

ANDREWS: Yes.

GOTTLIEB: But this is true of all men. For company they prefer males. I can sense it in myself. I have very few, if any, female friends whom I could call for a social, nonsexual evening. There are very few women whose company I like. I would prefer to talk to you or to another male—discuss politics, sports, philosophize, even gossip—with a man.

ANDREWS: David, you very sharply just blurred the distinction between the homosexual way and the heterosexual way. It seems that we gays are more homosocials than homosexuals, aren't we? When the homosexual wishes to spend time with males without any sexuality, that seems crazy because you said, David, that if you spend time with a heterosexual woman, sex would probably be part of that meeting. Here you have the homosexual male grouping where sex is always available and yet most gays deal with each other on a nonsexual basis. They're selecting their own gender because it's easier to identify with them. This brings up a lot of other conditioning factors. Remember that all of us are subject to the idea that there are certain things you don't say or do in front of members of the opposite sex. You have more freedom and comfort with your own sex. There is really hardly anything more bawdy than a bunch of women together.

Homosociality crosses the straight-gay barrier. We men prefer the company of our own sex in social situations. We are freer with one another and we can say things we would not say in front of women. We do not have to mind our manners; we are secure with our own kind. We share the male conspiracy.

I am homosocial when I prefer male to female company. Straight men who prefer platonic women friends give me a creepy feeling. These men carry themselves as if their penises will fall off in any intense social or professional encounter with real men, gay or straight. They literally avoid men. They are ladies' men and as much as possible avoid the brotherhood of homosociality.

From the confusion of trying to define homosexual comes the clarity of a new term—homosocial—a link between people of the same gender, no matter how far apart their sexual preferences are.

Epilogue

I felt myself changing as I worked on this. My old attitude toward gays is no longer what it was before we began our talks. This became most obvious when Andrews turned the tables and started questioning me.

ANDREWS: You say there has been a shift in your attitude toward gays. What is the shift? Let's say during the ten-year period since I talked to you and you wanted me to get myself straightened out.

GOTTLIEB: I've come to accept the fact that in the majority of situations gays don't come to see me in order to become like me. They don't want to be "straightened out."

ANDREWS: How long did it take you to realize that?

GOTTLIEB: I think probably three or four years of working with gays. In my own psychoanalytic training the question never really came up.

ANDREWS: Never?

GOTTLIEB: Never came up in terms of analyzing somebody. Put it this way. The purpose of a classic psychoanalysis is to have a person reach a level of genital-sexual relationships, which means heterosexual relationships. If a gay came to see an analyst, the assumption was that he wanted to become heterosexual.

ANDREWS: Do you think that past attitude was coupled with a condescending attitude in the orthodox psychiatric sense?

GOTTLIEB: On my part, yes. My work here and my work with some gay patients gave me a depth of understanding which I frankly did not have before. I suppose in that respect this work is very therapeutic for me in terms of my...

ANDREWS: Is it a wash? Is it therapeutic for you or do you find yourself becoming a psychoanalytic, straight male equivalent of a fag hag?

GOTTLIEB: No! No! No!

ANDREWS: Maybe you're enchanted with the gays as exotic...

GOTTLIEB: No. There is something that precedes that. It is that I, like most straights, would have had an aversion to the concept of homosexuality for myself.

ANDREWS: Yes?

GOTTLIEB: It's not an easy thing for me to describe to you, just the fear of it. It's an unknown kind of thing. Psychiatrists try to understand how a gay feels without having experienced being gay.

ANDREWS: I understand.

GOTTLIEB: I remember my own "normal" homosexuality between eight and thirteen—curiosity about other boys' bodies, who's got the biggest penis and how big an erection is. Curiosity and mutual masturbation are considered perfectly normal at that age, but when you get older you repress the memory of those childhood activities. Then it is difficult to empathize with the gay. Then it can be threatening.

ANDREWS: Well, between empathy and identity there's a big gap, but it's subtle.

GOTTLIEB: Yes.

ANDREWS: And I wonder if a lot of therapists and analysts don't confuse the meanings of these words.

GOTTLIEB: Yes.

ANDREWS: They are fearful of identifying and becoming...

GOTTLIEB: Yes. When I was a resident in psychiatry I wrote one of the first papers on the psychotherapeutic treatment of a retarded child. I was asked why I wanted to work with stupid people, the implication being that I was stupid like my patient. It happens to have been an excellent paper and I put it on a shelf and never published it for the simple reason that down deep I was kind of ashamed of it. I should have been dealing with the gifted child. Subsequently there was a great interest in retardation. Enormous sums of money were put into the study of mental retardation and it became respectable. In retrospect, I should have published the paper.

ANDREWS: But homosexuality is abhorrent to the psychiatrist.

GOTTLIEB: It was abhorrent to me, and I could not work effectively. I went back trying to apply what I had learned, my techniques, over and over again. They had to work! How could someone prefer boys to girls? How could a male not feel as I do? I was not using empathy. I felt it would compromise my masculinity because gays, I thought, were antimasculine. But they're not. So now I'm comfortable with them as males.

ANDREWS: David, you now accept gays as males, swell, but you've also told me that true bisexuality is rare. Would you now agree that there can be straight bisexuals and gay bisexuals if only at moments?

GOTTLIEB: If you are referring, Andy, to a normal bisexuality in all of us, I agree—and so did Freud. But the person who has sexual relations either way, anytime, without discretion, is usually very disturbed. Too many male homosexuals call themselves bisexuals because it sounds better. Actually they're labeling themselves as very sick people.

Being candid means being honest enough to show one's inconsistencies and changes of opinion. I would never have guessed, when I approached these discussions, that my attitude toward homosexuals would change as it has. I believe I can safely assume that my collaborators also changed some of their opinions and attitudes during their frank conversations with me. I hope that this work will answer questions, broaden attitudes, break down simplistic stereotypes, and provide new insights for the reader—straight and gay.